RAISING A BODY-CONFIDENT DAUGHTER

DANNAH GRESH
FOUNDER OF TRUE GIRL

HARVEST HOUSE PUBLISHERS
EUGENE, OREGON

Cover photo © Mr_Twister / Getty Images; JGI / Jaimie Grill / Blend Images / fotosearch
Cover design by Bryce Williamson
Interior design by KUHN Design Group

For bulk, special sales, or ministry purchases, please call 1 800 547 8979.
Email: Customerservice@hhpbooks.com

M is a federally registered trademark of the Hawkins Children's LLC.
Harvest House Publishers, Inc., is the exclusive licensee of the trademark.

TRUE GIRL is a trademark of Dannah Gresh.

Raising a Body-Confident Daughter
Copyright © 2015 by Dannah Gresh
Published by Harvest House Publishers
Eugene, Oregon 97408
www.harvesthousepublishers.com

ISBN 978-0-7369-8193-4 (pbk.)
ISBN 978-0-7369-8194-1 (eBook)

The Library of Congress has cataloged the edition as follows:

Library of Congress Cataloging-in-Publication Data
    Gresh, Dannah, 1967-
    Raising body-confident daughters / Dannah Gresh.
    pages cm — (8 Great Dates)
    ISBN 978-0-7369-6005-2 (pbk.)
    ISBN 978-0-7369-6006-9 (eBook)
    1. Mothers and daughters—Religious aspects—Christianity. 2. Body image in girls—Religious aspects—Christianity. 3. Girls—Religious life. I. Title.
    BV4529.18.G7425 2015
    248.8'431—dc23
            2014028523

Printed in the United States of America

21 22 23 24 25 26 27 28 29 / BP / 10 9 8 7 6 5 4 3 2 1

*Grow in grace and in the knowledge of
our Lord and Savior Jesus Christ.*

2 Peter 3:18

A BIG SQUEEZE TO:

If you're one of the more than a million moms and daughters who have participated in one of our True Girl online Bible studies, attended a live True Girl event, or used one of our printed resources to get closer to each other and to Jesus, I wish I could hug you right now. (I've loved getting to know you through Instagram and Facebook.) Every time you show up, you are standing with me to say that what God instructs about womanhood matters. Thank you!

I also want to thank Harvest House Publishers for partnering with us for the exciting growth of True Girl. This publishing house is built on the Word of God…literally. A copy of the Bible is buried in the foundation of the building to remind them what matters. And that matters to me. I'm especially grateful to Barb Sherrill and Gene Skinner, who have been indispensable as we figure out how to meet the needs of all those True Girls.

It seems fitting to also thank Suzy Weibel, since a few paragraphs in this book started in a book that she wrote, but I ended up stealing them (with her permission) for this book! Suzy never complains when we strategize like this and change things—she just trusts Jesus and me. What a good friend!

Eileen King, for plowing the ground for me to write. She creates the fertile soil of time by taking the weight of many things off my back so I can get away from the office and write until my fingers are sore! I'm sure hers are too. This book came from her heart as much as mine!

While I'm at the task of squeezing, I'm so grateful for my main squeeze, Bob. True Girl was his idea, and he has been a faithful visionary and CEO. Bob has married administrative genius and patience to lead us through 15 marvelous years of bringing girls and their moms closer to each other and to God.

Mostly, thanks to Jesus, whom I long to be with every day. May my body be his living sacrifice.

—Dannah

CONTENTS

— — —

WHY YOUR DAUGHTER NEEDS BODY CONFIDENCE

I met sweet Hannah Banana—excuse my tendency to nickname everyone I meet—when she was about eight, but I'd seen her picture long before I met her. She was a model for the cover of a music CD as a tween girl. In the close-up photo, her eyes were closed in worship as she tilted her head boldly to the sky, sending a contented smile in heaven's direction. Her skin was naked—free from any kind of makeup, including powder or lip gloss. In stark contrast to a picture-perfect world, her beauty did not come from perfection on the outside but something internal.

But this was just a photo, right?

Wrong.

Real-life Hannah, who was athletic and nearly always in basketball shorts and a T-shirt because she just didn't care what she wore, *always* had that look on her face. Contagious peace. Her beauty came from deep within.

Imagine my absolute shock when, several years after meeting her, I learned something that might have kept her from exuding so much confidence. Hannah was missing most of her fingers on her left hand. I noticed it the day she came to school with her arm in a cast from a recent break. I was so shocked, I gasped and asked if her hand was swollen, thinking maybe that was why her fingers looked short. But they just weren't there! I had never noticed. More importantly, Hannah didn't seem to notice either. She typed, played basketball, wrote papers, and cooked—all with a significant handicap but also with exquisite natural beauty and total confidence. Today she is a young woman in her first job as a teacher. She remains rather makeup free and unconcerned with what she wears, but she is as breathtaking as ever.

Contrast her to a girl we will just call Jane. I saw a photo of her before I met her too. Her features were flawless. Perfectly crafted nose, full lips, gorgeous deep brown eyes, and dark skin. But there was no smile on her face. Just a hollow stare that hid her beauty. I remember wondering what could possibly have made her sad enough to wear such a haunted look on her face.

When I met her as a preteen, fear was etched all over her, though it was somewhat ebbed by (of all things) shopping. A smile or giggle would sneak through from time to time, but her face primarily remained in that state of haunted beauty. Buying clothes seemed to make this tween forget her insecurities. Experimenting with makeup was fun at first but soon seemed to be *necessary*. An obsession with name brands led to a spending problem. I strongly suspect an eating disorder set in sometime during her teen years. Today she is a skeleton of a young women with little life direction. She cakes herself with makeup that makes her look like a clown, she's literally ashamed if she's not wearing brand-name clothes, and she can't look in the mirror without crying on a daily basis.

What's the difference between Hannah and Jane? Hannah has body confidence, and Jane suffers from body consciousness.

You may have picked up this book to help your daughter be more like Hannah and less like Jane. Will your daughter struggle with an eating disorder or use food as her fuel? Will she use exercise to beat her body into a skeletal size or use it to make her strong for her life call? Will she look in the mirror with self-loathing or with confidence? These are reasonable concerns for a mom raising a girl in our body-conscious society—and good reasons to be a mom who coaches your daughter into body confidence.

What Is Body Consciousness?

Consciousness is the awareness of an external object or something within oneself. Simply put, anything we are aware of at a specific moment is something about which we are conscious.

Body consciousness is the state of being constantly aware of the body— either others' or your own, but mostly your own. It can include obsession with clothing and makeup, nonstop surveillance of the appearance of others or yourself, deep body shame, sexualization of self or others, and unending appearance management. (Can't walk by a mirror without checking yourself? You might have some issues with body consciousness! Don't worry, friend. We'll tackle our own junk in this book too.)

Our society idolizes the body. Everything is about how we look and who is beautiful. Of course, beauty is often determined by a makeup palette, designer-name brands, and a little Photoshop magic. When we stop to consider the messages that perpetuate this plague, we find they are motivated by another idol—the almighty dollar. People can become rich by creating a society in which our appearance matters more than anything else. And if manufacturers, retailers, and marketers start early, they'll have "cradle to grave" customers. That's why our girls are at risk *now*!

In recent years, retailers have rolled out everything from thong underwear called Eye Candy to padded bikini-top bras for girls aged eight to twelve. Eyeliner and mascara sales for this age group doubled. (Someone tell me why little girls need those products!) I believe Christians need to remain positive and avoid boycotting when possible, but I've helped moms to gently but unflinchingly confront retail giants that peddle products that make our daughters grow up too fast.

Unfortunately, only a tiny minority of moms are concerned about these issues.

Girls aged eight to twelve spend about $500 million a year on beauty products alone.[1] At least one brand now markets its make up to girls as young as four. As long as moms let their daughters keep spending, marketers will continue targeting this age group. *It's all about money.* Once when I was crying out publicly for awareness regarding this, I was interviewed by *Women's Wear Daily*, the global bible of the fashion industry.

At that time, I was leading 25,000 concerned moms who had recently selected three retailers that consistently provide age-appropriate clothing and products for our daughters. We agreed to arm ourselves with time and money and Shop till We Drop in an effort to say thanks to these outlets. (It was a reverse boycott. We were sending a message in a positive way.) The media covered our event, and I was thrilled.

In a round of phone tag, one of my team members asked a reporter, "What will it take for the industry to start caring about what it's doing to our daughters?"

The reporter replied, "They don't care. It's all about money to them. You shouldn't take it personally. It's just a financial thing."

I take it very personally. And so should you, because the stakes are incredibly high!

The Risks of Body Consciousness

A two-year study by the American Psychological Association Task Force on the Sexualization of Girls (a title that has the stench of body consciousness) revealed that products and marketing that target tween girls are linked to eating disorders, low self-esteem, depression, and early sexual activity.[2] (Read: They create body consciousness.) Isn't it ironic that instead of making girls feel good about their bodies, all these "beauty" products make our daughters—and sometimes us—feel fat or unattractive? Body consciousness will not serve your daughter well. Here are the two big overriding risks of body-conscious living.

Body consciousness creates a hyperawareness of every flaw, unique beauty mark, or divergence from the media's norm of beauty. This hyperawareness influences the way your daughter cares for herself and can be lethal. For example, consider the way tween girls think about food. The *Washington Post* has lamented the growing number of younger and younger patients at eating disorder clinics around the nation.

"A decade ago, new eating disorder patients at Children's National Medical Center tended to be around age 15," says

Adelaide Robb, director of inpatient psychiatry. "Today kids come in as young as 5 and 6."[3]

Low self-esteem, depression, and an early sexual debut—which are all related to what our girls believe about their bodies and their beauty—are big risks when our girls become victims of body consciousness. Before we know it, hyperawareness of a crooked tooth or a zit becomes an excuse for cutting or drives our once-giggling girls into a deep depression. It has to stop!

More harmful still, body consciousness creates an extreme focus on the body at the expense of your daughter's spirit. Children are supposed to be learning right from wrong between the ages of eight and ten, not how to accessorize an outfit or put on mascara. They should be learning to live healthy emotional, mental, and spiritual lives, not getting lost in tween dating drama or competitive unofficial beauty contests at school. If they fall prey to society's body-conscious norms, they will become overly focused on their external beauty, often at the expense of tending to their spirit.

Consider this—the average (that is, normal) person between the ages of nine and seventeen scores as high on anxiety scales as children who were admitted to psychological clinics for severe disorders in the 1950s. We simply have not been tending to the spirits of our children or teaching them the art of tending their own spirits. (All the while, their name-brand duds are often picture perfect!)

What Is Body Confidence?

It's time to push the reset button, but take care how you do so. It's not that your daughter's body is bad. In fact, her valuable but temporal body houses her eternal spirit, and if she has a relationship with Jesus Christ, it is the temple of God. Her body is good and useful, which brings us to the definition of body confidence.

Confidence is full trust in or reliability of people or things. It's being able to depend on things or people to do what they are supposed to do.

Body confidence is the awareness of your body's purpose and ability to depend on it to do what God designed it to do without making too much or too little of it. When our thoughts about our bodies are based on God's intended purpose, we experience God-esteem, not self-esteem. And if we esteem God, we will understand the great value of our bodies without making too much of them.

Here's the key. As you teach your daughter to confidently care for her body, emphasize the care of her spirit and teach her to press in to godliness. Of course, we can't give our daughters what we don't have. This book will give you what you need to move your daughter away from body consciousness and its risks and toward the glorious beauty of body confidence. But I have to warn you, we're going to dive in headfirst to make sure that you and I have shaken off every bit of our own body consciousness and are learning to wear the beauty that comes with body confidence.

Trust me, you're gonna like how this feels!

> *While bodily training is of some value, godliness is of value in every way, as it holds promise for the present life and also for the life to come (1 Timothy 4:8).*

2

STARTING WITH YOU

How do you feel about *your* body today?

I told you we would be taking care of you too. And the fact is, how you feel about your body will impact how your daughter feels about hers. Over and over I've counseled teens or college-age girls who realized that their self-loathing started with their mothers' dissatisfaction with themselves. Conversely, a popular Dove campaign revealed that girls felt confident about their bodies when their moms felt confident about their own. For example, one mom confessed that she didn't really love the shape and size of her legs, but she chose to focus on the fact that they were strong and good for running rather than the negatives she sometimes felt. Her daughter, not knowing what her mom had told interviewers, said that she liked her own legs "because they're good for running."[4]

So, let me ask again, how do you feel about *your* body today?

Is it strong and useful and well-presented?

Me? Strong and useful—check. But well-presented? Hmm... depends on what you mean by "presented." Honestly, I'm holed up in a hotel pounding out this book for you, and I may have just frightened the man who delivered my pizza moments ago. I feel fairly certain I should take a shower before I let the rest of the world see me. But here's the thing—I took care of my body today so I could do what God has designed me to do here and now. After a long weekend of ministry, I had to beat it into submission this Monday morning. I popped on my running shoes and workout clothes and went for a little jog and did some Pilates because I did not feel like living today. I needed a kick start. For my morning fuel I chose some eggs and toast and a hearty dose of caffeine at Denny's, and I'm now treating myself to a pizza for lunch because I've already worked it off. (For dinner, I guess I'll have to get some protein and greens.) I feel *great* about my body today and how I presented it to God this morning for his usefulness even though I'm not the cutest I've ever been sitting here in my workout clothes.

How about you? Do you feel good in your skin today? Did you take care of your body and present it to God for his use today? Or are you confused about how to feel good about your own body, let alone how to raise your daughter to feel that way?

Let's start at the beginning, shall we? In order to be confident in your body's purpose, you have to know what that purpose is!

I Am a Woman

I am a woman.

I know this is true because I have breasts and ovaries. I carry XX chromosomes. I can produce ovum or egg cells—female *gametes*, if you want to get scientific. These factors and others make me a woman. They are a few of the standards by which we judge our biological sex.

Before 1955, I would not have needed to put the word "biological" before "sex." Until then, there was a simplistic understanding of binary gender. Obviously, we've learned that this conversation hurt a lot of people who were struggling to identify with their anatomy for one reason or another. And then one simple word was introduced, and while it's been helpful to some as they seek answers to their confusion, it's also created ample confusion for others.

What word was introduced? "Gender."

Sexologist John Money introduced it to distinguish between biological sex and the way people prefer to play out their sexual identity. It really didn't catch on until the 1970s, when the feminist movement grabbed on to it and held tight in their efforts to break down the differentiation between masculinity and femininity.

It's been quite a ride ever since.

Recently, the media is full of applause for stunning women (athletes, actresses, politicians…), but they aren't. They are men who dress and act like women because they feel they are female. One admittedly liberal writer of an article on the topic was confused and admitted struggling to wrap her mind around the situation. She questioned whether there should possibly be some sort of plumb line for gender.[5]

I know, I know.

This chapter probably seems like more than you bargained for in a book that's supposed to help you teach your daughter body confidence. You picked it up to get some practical help in talking to your daughter about washing her hair and the arrival of her period. But how can we talk about her body unless we first have a foundation of what her body tells her about who she is? What *does* it mean to be female? Does she like being a girl? Do you?

Let's start here: God *chose* for you to be a woman. Of course, regardless of the monthly cramps you dislike so much, or the glass ceiling that bumped you in the head, or the confusion you may have faced about being a woman, God chose this for you. (Not the cramps or the glass ceiling or the confusion. Each of those is a result of the Fall, not his intentional design.) The question many of us are left with is, why did he choose this for you? The answer to this question is the foundation for *body confidence.*

Of course, entire books have been written on this complex subject, and if your questions are complicated or if you or your daughter are heartbroken by gender identity challenges, you'll need to get some of them. But may I offer a condensed theology of the body for you to consider?

In the beginning, God laid a foundation for the questions we'd face about our bodies. It's recorded in the story of creation.

> *Then God said, "Let us make man in our image, after our likeness…" So God created man in his own image, in the image of*

God he created him; male and female he created them (Genesis 1:26-27).

We'll root four statements about our bodies in this verse. I hope it will affirm you or help you grow in your understanding of *why* God made our bodies the way he chose.

1. Every human being is created in the image of God. You have incredible intrinsic value. (Oh, if only we could live with a strong sense of our worth!) God is the author of human essence. You did not come into being by accident. He desired you and designed you. It was his great pleasure to bring you into existence. This fact of our creation is a vital source of understanding what it means to be human.

As I write this, I have an urgent sense that we've forgotten this incredible truth. We would not need a book on body confidence for our girls if it were not a battle to believe that we have great worth. Genesis 1:26-27 declares this value four times as it summarizes a conversation between God the Father, God the Son, and God the Holy Spirit:

- "Let us make man in *our image*,"

- "after *our likeness*..."

- "So God created man in *his own image*,"

- "*in the image of God* he created him."

He sure wanted it to be clear. I guess he knew we'd get amnesia and forget who we are. I beg you to remember. Let your own soul soak in the truth that you are created in the image of God.

2. Our primary purpose is to glorify God. The fact that we were made in his image means we were made to glorify him. That is, to point to and look like him. God made you for that reason and has jealously protected this purpose by sacrificing his Son. This should motivate us to participate in the essence of glorifying him. And it takes our bodies to do this.

You were bought with a price. So glorify God in your body
(1 Corinthians 6:20).

If your heart is thirsty and confused and wearied by religion, you most likely haven't discovered the power of your true purpose: to glorify God in your body. This is not a dull and dutiful existence. Rather, as you discover and surrender to God's intension to be glorified through you, you'll be swept away with passion and infused with true joy. This sensation is probably best stated in a famous quote from the Westminster Confession.

The chief end of man is to glorify God and enjoy him forever.

It is one chief end—to glorify and to enjoy. The surrender and the sometimes hard work of glorifying him with your body are married to the treasure of being in a state of pleasure. These two things cannot be separated. I have heard no better way to say it than the way Pastor John Piper does in *Desiring God* when he calls himself a Christian hedonist. You will experience the greatest pleasure of your life when you finally find the way the puzzle piece of your purpose fits into the great picture of God's plan.

3. Our primary practice, then, must be to look like him, and we do that best in his defined roles of maleness and femaleness. After the Godhead states and then restates three times that we exist to glorify him, the Scriptures record that he created us "male and female."

Humanity possesses so many God-like qualities. Why doesn't God mention the traits of being intelligent or worshipful or creative when he says we were created in his image? Why doesn't he commend our language proficiency or our ability to compose sonnets? Apparently, these are not the things that make us most like a representation of God. Our maleness and our femaleness make us like him. This places authentic humanity and sexuality in the context of male and female distinctiveness. Our ability to look like him mandates that we embrace those differences, not erase them.

Romans 1 teaches us that disregarding God's definitions of manhood and womanhood is a rebellious refusal to glorify him and an attempt to hide who he is and *whose* we are. Pastor John Piper puts it this way:

> God's divine nature is revealed in the physical, material universe. So much so that verse 20 says, "So they are without excuse" when they "exchange the glory of God for the glory of the creature" (verse 23), or when they "exchange the truth about God for a lie and worship and serve the creature rather than the Creator" (verse 25).
>
> Paul is saying that the material, physical universe reveals God's true nature, and his design for humans to worship him.
>
> Then Paul draws the parallel with human sexuality. Just as physical nature reveals the truth about God, so physical nature reveals truth about sexual identity. *Whom* we should worship is not left to our preferences, and *who we are* sexually is not left to our preferences. Both are dictated by God's revelation in nature…
>
> The parallel Paul is making is this: On the one hand, cosmology is designed by God to reveal truth about *God's* identity (as powerful and divine); on the other hand, biology (anatomy) is designed by God to reveal truth about *our* identity (as male and female). This truth is so plain, Paul says, that we are "without excuse" if we don't see it and agree with it.[6]

4. Our bodies, therefore, must be a living sacrifice to God. The Christian vision of gender is complex, and the Scriptures do not ignore the fact that it will be difficult for some. In Romans 12, the apostle Paul begs for us to lay down our own desires, thoughts, and plans for our bodies and to make them daily, living, breathing sacrifices so we can fulfill our purpose of glorifying God. This includes how we work, live, give, spend, and even whom we have sex with and how we think about our gender.

> *I appeal to you therefore… by the mercies of God, to present your bodies as a living sacrifice, holy and acceptable to God, which is your spiritual worship. Do not be conformed to this world, but be transformed by the renewal of your mind, that by testing you may discern what is the will of God, what is good and acceptable and perfect (Romans 12:1-3).*

Why did God make you a woman?

Because you were created to contribute to humanity's purpose of glorifying and enjoying God, and God chose for you to do that as a woman. You illuminate who God is when you embrace the role of womanhood because it is in male and female distinctions that we are the image of God. Sometimes, this will be a sacrifice for you.

Will you give of yourself?

Before you answer, let me remind you: Christ surrendered his body for you. A love relationship with him invites us to return the gift.

If you're not there yet, it's okay. I'm certainly more confident and compassionate about my convictions concerning a theology of my body than I once was. In fact, my desire to help girls and their moms grow in their understanding of their bodies was birthed out of the sting of my own body-conscious living. At the very young age of 15, I found myself giving my body to a teenage boy *in large part because I had very little confidence of any kind*! Oh, what pain followed! But I have experienced the greatest depth of God's love and healing and have entered into a rich understanding of the worth and purpose of my body. Each time I get to help a girl or mom, God is continuing his wonderful act of restoring my soul—and my body—to its rightful place.

Since Christ began his healing work in me, my heart has never been the same. It became one big megaphone as I pleaded to God for the hearts of daughters—first my own, then countless others, and now yours. This book is my invitation to you to shout out to God along with me for our girls. But doing that is kind of like flying in an airplane.

(Pardon the whiplash-like shift in analogies, but I'm sitting with a view of the Orlando International Airport out my hotel room, and this just came to me.) Girlfriend, you've got to put on your own oxygen mask before you can put one on your daughter.

Do you know why God made you to be a woman?

Do you understand your purpose?

> *The Lord will fulfill his purpose for me;*
>   *your steadfast love, O Lord, endures forever.*
>   *Do not forsake the work of your hands (Psalm 138:8).*

3

HELPING YOUR DAUGHTER TO BE BODY CONFIDENT

"Mom, can I shave?"

"Mom, why is everyone in my class buying bras?"

"Mom, when will I get my period?"

"Mom, is kissing okay?"

If your daughter is feeling body confident and safe, she's going to ask a lot of questions related to her body between the ages of eight and twelve. Of course, the questions are direct and frequent if she is an extrovert, and they're a bit muted and rarely spoken out loud if she is an introvert. Nonetheless, they exist.

Meanwhile, other people are beginning to ask questions about her body too.

Your doctor may ask you if you will sign papers to have your daughter receive vaccination against sexually transmitted diseases. Boys who think she's cute may be asking if they can date her very soon. School nurses might inquire about her weight...or lack thereof. How do I know these questions will come? They came to this mom's heart when my girls were tweens. And they will come to yours too.

> If you do not plant truth in your daughter about her body, her value system will be formed by the world and not the Word.

A mom cannot sit by passively, just allowing everything to happen. You have to be intentional about leading her into womanhood, and you have to begin now, while she is so very young. I wrote this in *Six Ways to Keep the "Little" in Your Girl*:

> This is when her values are formed, not when she is a teenager. If you've waited until she is 12 to tell her about her period, you'll have missed the beauty of telling her that God created women to create life and that's *why* we value motherhood. If you wait until she's 13 to tell her about modesty, you'll have missed the beauty of telling her *why* her body is good and beautiful and worthy of protecting. If you wait until she's 14 to tell her about sex, you'll have missed the beauty of telling her *why* God created marriage to be a one man–one woman picture of his love for us. It's not that you won't be able to try to form her values after she's 13. It's just that the world will have already issued a fairly strong answer to the "why's" in her heart if you haven't, and restructuring her value system is a lot more difficult than building it from the ground up…
>
> Introducing critical subjects after the age of 12 is like kayaking upstream! Your daughter's belief system is already formed, and introducing values in her teens—when she's no longer asking *why*—is difficult! So the question for you now—in her tweens—is not "*Should* I talk to her about boys, and sex, and periods, and other stuff that scares me silly?" The question is "*How* do I talk to her about boys, and sex, and periods, and other stuff that scares me silly *without robbing her of her innocence?*" I think I can help you with this.

Your daughter needs to hear truth—the standard or original by which she can judge her value as a woman—from you. Not school. Not a book. Not the Disney channel. You.

That's why I've developed these eight conversations for you to have with your daughter. They'll cover some of the most important information. There are three basic topics we'll cover.

Becoming a Woman

I got my period one month after my twelfth birthday. It was a positive experience despite a few of life's most embarrassing mishaps, which I'll happily tell you about privately in person one day. But many of the women I've interviewed on this topic had very unhappy stories to tell because they had no idea why there was blood in their panties! Imagine the fear. (Well, maybe you can.) Forty percent of women start their periods without having heard about it from their own parents.[7]

Sometime between her ninth and thirteenth birthday, your daughter is going to start her period. Let's make sure her memory of that first time is positive and sets her up for lifelong understanding, not dread. I'll share with you a method I developed and used with my girls that gave them a more positive outlook on the whole thing. (Think: chocolate.)

And while getting her period is the most significant *external* marker of her womanhood, building *internal* markers of truth for her is critical if she is to understand what God says about being a girl.

Body Care

In the beginning of sixth grade, I had a friend we'll call Wendy. It was a most unnatural friendship, forced by my mom, who was wiggling her way into my classroom to try to help the poor girl. Wendy had the greasiest hair imaginable and particularly strong body odor. She was also known to show up in school with a tight spaghetti-strap top shamelessly hugging her tiny breast buds. (Often coupled with satin shorts and high heels.) Poor, sweet girl. I didn't know that her mom had died when she was younger. Evidently her dad was just terrified of her changing body, so he had asked my mom to help.

SMALL-GROUP ALTERNATIVE

As we delve into topics of womanhood and gender, it's imperative to build positive peer pressure among the girls in your church, school, or community. You might encourage some mother-daughter pairs to have these conversations "with" you. You'll still do them all alone, but you'll have two or three mothers taking their daughters through them at basically the same pace so you can talk about it and enjoy it together. (It might be fun for the moms to meet for lunch now and then to update and encourage one another!) And the challenge activity for conversation two—a girls' night out—would be really great as a small-group activity with all the moms and daughters together!

By the end of sixth grade, Wendy's hair was well-groomed, her armpits had been introduced to deodorant, and my mom had built up enough emotional capital to commandeer the spaghetti-strap top. And Wendy became a great friend to me too—a friend who just needed a mom to help her learn to take care of her body.

No girl knows how to take care of her body on her own. And the risks include more than just social stigma. With childhood and teen obesity dramatically rising in the past three decades, we need to teach our daughters how to exercise and eat healthy by informing them and helping them form good habits. I'll share with you some very fun ways to approach this.

Sex

Yep, it's time.

Approximately 50 percent of 16-year-old girls are sexually active, and there's very little statistical difference between our Christian kids and those from non-Christian homes. So much of the risk extends back to their tween years, when girls jump on the boy-crazy train. In the survey of 1,200 Christian teens Nancy DeMoss Wolgemuth and I conducted before writing *Lies Young Women Believe*, I was heartbroken to find just how dependent Christian girls are on guys. Regardless of whether Christian girls were in public schools or private schools or were being homeschooled, 68 percent said they'd be happier if they had a boyfriend.

One of the greatest ways to reduce the risk is to talk about it when she's ready. I've read material from just about every Christian psychologist or family expert out there, and they all agree that this talk needs to take place much earlier than we parents are generally comfortable having it. Dr. James Dobson, for example, says, "Sometime between six and nine, depending on the maturity and interest of an individual (and what is being heard in the neighborhood), he or she ought to understand how conception occurs."[8] Don't let that terrify you. Instead, let it inform and fuel you so you can do what God has entrusted you to do—build a value system with the foundation of the Word.

Eight Conversations You Must Have

I've used the four foundational truths of theology of our body and these three critical areas of concern to develop eight conversations you can have with your daughter. Each of the following chapters unfolds some thoughts for you on an important topic and then provides a creative, interactive, conversational "challenge activity" to have with your daughter. (Think: moon walks and girls' night out.) You are going to have *fun* teaching her these things! You'll explore the practical aspects of body care with her and plant a deep understanding of truth concerning her body. (And possibly enjoy a wonderful pedicure or girls' night out along the way!)

You can have these conversations during a weekly date together or spread them out and enjoy them as you are able to schedule them into your life. Just don't let them get too far apart. Here's an overview.

Conversation One: Your Body, a Purpose

Challenge activity: A Moon Walk
Key verse: 1 Corinthians 6:20
Key thought: Your body was created to glorify God.
Suggested challenge setting: a mountain,
field, beach, or observatory

— — —

Conversation Two: Your Body, Its Practice

Challenge activity: A Girls' Night Out
Key verse: Genesis 1:27
Key thought: God made girls to reflect his image.
Suggested challenge setting: a fun place to eat
out, like a teahouse or sports club

— — —

Conversation Three: Your Body, God's Temple

Challenge activity: A Body-Boosting Bubble Bath
Key verse: 1 Corinthians 3:16-17
Key thought: Your body is the temple of the Holy Spirit.
Suggested challenge setting: a Jacuzzi tub at a
hotel, Grandma's, or your own house

— — —

Conversation Four: Your Hair, a Crown

Challenge activity: A New "Do"!
Key verse: 1 Corinthians 11:15
Key thought: Even your hair can honor God.
Suggested challenge setting: a beauty salon
or an at-home salon experience

Conversation Five: Food, Your Fuel

Challenge activity: Salad and Smoothie Making 101
Key verse: Genesis 1:29
Key thought: God wants me to take care of my body when I eat.
Suggested challenge setting: a kitchen
Special needs: a blender

— — —

Conversation Six: Exercise, Your Strength

Challenge activity: An Exercise Challenge
Key verse: 1 Corinthians 9:27
Key thought: God wants me to take care
of my body with exercise.
Suggested challenge setting: a mountain, beach,
or walking trail in your neighborhood

— — —

Conversation Seven: Your Body, a Source of Life

Challenge activity: Death by Chocolate
Key verse: John 16:21
Key thought: Your body is empowered to create life.
Suggested challenge setting: a chocolate factory, a fondue
restaurant, or a chocolate fountain at home

— — —

Conversation Eight: Your Body, a Sacrifice

Challenge activity: A Career Day
Key verse: Romans 12:1-2
Key thought: Your body must be a living sacrifice.
Suggested challenge setting: an office or career
setting that is of interest to your daughter

FOR MORE HELP...

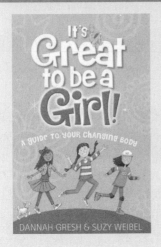

Raising body-confident daughters is not easy. It takes lots of repetition to get your daughter to believe God's truth concerning body confidence while the world is proselytizing her with body consciousness. So I have a related Bible study titled *It's Great to Be a Girl* for your daughter. My best friend, Former True Girl lead teacher Suzy Weibel, and I wrote it together.

Well, that's pretty much it. Ready to start thinking about your first conversation?

4

CONVERSATION ONE

YOUR BODY, A PURPOSE

Now I'm writing to you from my parents' little mountain house, where I've written at least a few pages of every book since the first one, *And the Bride Wore White*, in 2000. This is also a place where my family has written many memories. Three feet in front of me and to my right is the telescope that my wonderful dad set up in hopes that we'd all do some stargazing up here, where the sky is so black that I'm the only one who will sleep up here alone. Oh, how the stars shine, which is why we have camped out up here when God uses the sky to show off a bit.

The best memory we have of this place was the Leonid shower of 2001. Here's what I wrote in the guest book:

> Dan, Kay, Bob, Dannah, Rob, and Lexi all spent the night. After a rousing round of Pit, our first family attempt, we snuggled into bed for a nap. At four a.m. we rose to watch the heavens' light show—the annual Leonid meteor shower. We counted 18 in just 60 seconds at one point. Beautiful! Then back to bed to sleep in! (P.S. Grampy found fresh claw marks on the front of the house this morning.)

Lexi's version was a bit more concise.

We saw falling stars. It was cool. We slept in the cabin.

My daughter still remembers that night. And so do I.

Oh, my friend, the conversation I want you to have with your daughter to plant the truth of this chapter must be memorable. After all, we're going to present a lesson she must never forget.

Your daughter's primary purpose in life
is to glorify God and to enjoy him.

In order to glorify him, we must live a God-centered life. Pastor John Piper has devoted his life to teaching the church to glorify God. He warns us, "Many people are willing to be God-centered as long as they feel God is man-centered. It is a subtle danger. We may think we are centering our lives on God when we are really making Him a means to self-esteem."[9]

Oh, how guilty of this I am. I so want to believe that God wants me to be happy, but his goal is really to make me holy so I can illuminate his greatness. How very critical it is that you and I teach our children to override the egocentric world they're growing up in. If I read one more magazine article or parenting book that says our kids need self-esteem, I just may scream. Our children do not need self-esteem—they need God-esteem. If they have God-esteem, they will understand their value but not make too much of themselves. Instead, they will expend themselves, allowing the perfect image of God to be reflected through their lives.

Let's take our daughters past the shallow end of the living pool and go in deep, equipping them with a truth-drenched understanding of the purpose God assigns to each of us.

This conversation is going to include the world's biggest object lesson. Your tools? The moon and the sun. (I said it was big, didn't I?) Even though you'll be looking at the moon, it will be the sun's light that makes it glorious. And that's the whole point. After all, we have no light of our own. If not for the light of our Father, we would not shine in this dark world. The moon illuminates, or "glorifies," the sun. Get ready to teach your daughter what it means to glorify God by taking a late-night moon walk. Your conversation could go something like this.

Mom: Have you ever wondered where the moon gets its light?

Daughter: (She may know if she's studied it in school, in which case praise her and let her explain to you. If she needs help, make sure she understands how it works by continuing on.)

Mom: The moon has no light of its own. We would not see it if it were not for the sun. Each evening when our side of the earth turns away from the sun and toward the moon, it's like we have our back to the sun. We can't see it. But the sun's rays are so powerful that they travel right past the earth and hit the moon, making it bright and beautiful like it is tonight. (Draw the diagram below in the sand or dirt or on a piece of paper for your daughter to see as you share the information in this paragraph.)

Mom continues: The sun provides the light for our entire solar system. Everything on the planet reflects the light of the sun, or we would not see it at all. A rock, for example, would appear as a dark spot if it weren't for the sun. But nothing reflects it quite as grandly as the moon, does it?

Daughter: (Let her respond.)

Mom: In a way, the moon is "glorifying" the sun. The reflection of the sun on the moon illuminates the sun, or makes it known. The moon is saying, "Look at the sun!" It's reminding us that the sun is there even though we can't see it. That's kind of what it means to glorify God. The Bible teaches us that the most important thing you and I will ever do is to make God known or illuminate him. First Corinthians 6:19-20 says, "Do you not know that your body is a temple of the Holy Spirit within you, whom you have from God? You are not your own, for you were bought with a price. So glorify God in your body." Our bodies should be like the moon. We should constantly be saying, "Look at God!" What are some ways that we can do that?

Daughter: (She might say read her Bible or go to church, but try to get her past those things to character qualities that God gives us, such as love, joy, peace, patience, and so on. We must get beyond doing—performing actions that give us the hollow perception of glorifying him—and emphasize being—allowing him to shine out of us.)

Mom: Where do we learn to be like that?

Daughter: (She may say God or church, but remind her that the Holy Spirit, who is mentioned in our Bible verse, is the ultimate source.)

Mom: The Bible verse we're going to look at tonight tells us that the Holy Spirit teaches us to be kind or loving or joyful. So in a way, when we demonstrate those things, we are like the moon reflecting the sun's light. We're just reflecting the qualities of God to the world.

Remember, punctuate the conversation with an experience! My suggestion is to do it late at night.

To get this book into your hands, I deprived myself of many good nights' sleep. A few extra early mornings over a holiday weekend and all too many midnight-oil sessions enabled me to finally put it to bed. Speaking of which, I'll gladly retreat to bed should you pronounce a bedtime for me tonight.

But try to tell that to me when I was a tween.

Hardly a night went by that I didn't try to cheat bedtime least a tad. Sometimes I'd be outright visible, staying in the living room during my mother's many requests to retire. But most times I had a date with a flashlight under the covers, where my favorite fiction books were waiting for me.

My husband and I remembered the power of skipping bedtime when our kids were tweens, and we took advantage of it. Our son got Wing Nites with dad once a week at eight p.m., and you'd have thought he'd just been given permission to drive under age. But Wing Nites were not about staying up late. They were about planting biblical truth into his heart, which was fertile soil because he was so excited about missing bedtime.

Try to remember just how big a privilege staying up late can be when you're ten, and you'll understand the power of this mother–daughter challenge. And you need power for this one. You're about to share one of the Bible's greatest truths with her—that she exists to glorify God and to enjoy him.

PLANNING CONVERSATION ONE

A MOON WALK

Subject: your body and its purpose

Setting options: a mountain, field, beach, or observatory

Materials you'll need:

- A lunar calendar and weather report so you can find a night when the moon will be a spectacular sight. Schedule your conversation for that night and be willing to make last-minute changes should the weather not cooperate. It's imperative that you get a great moon-viewing night for this date.

- a telescope (optional)

- a late-night picnic (optional)

- a lantern or two flashlights

- this book

There are two goals during the challenge. The first is for your daughter to enjoy the thrill of being up past her bedtime and to enjoy a really special time with you. Pop out your snack pack and enjoy each other under the moonlight. There are ideas in the sidebar for moon walks in various seasons and climates.

The second goal is to have a conversation with her about the primary purpose of her body. You can use what I scripted out for you earlier in this chapter or make up your own conversation.

For the best results, present your daughter with her copy of *It's Great to Be a Girl*. Do meditation 1 together as part of your conversation or assign it as homework. If you do not have that book, you can discuss these things.

1. Read 1 Corinthians 6:19-20 and talk about the one thing God mentions we should use to glorify him. (Answer: body.)

2. Read 1 Corinthians 10:31. What two things are mentioned concerning what we do with our bodies that glorify God? (Answer: eating and drinking.)

3. The verse also says "whatever you do." What specific things can you add to this? Hint: What things do you do with your body? Anything you do should glorify him. (Possible answers: gymnastics, painting, how I dress, sleeping, who I like, dating, hugging, kissing...)

MOON WALK IDEAS AND RECIPES

A MIDSUMMER'S NIGHT

Indulge me the Shakespeare! Summer is a great setting for this conversation. Just grab a small cooler of icy lemonade and make these delightful cookies. You might want something salty to munch on, such as pretzels.

LEMON MOON COOKIES

These cookies will look like the moon, but they'll melt in your mouth like cotton candy. They have just a touch of lemony taste but are mostly a very sweet treat. My mom used to make these for me, and I love them.

1 pkg. lemon cake mix
2 cups Cool Whip
1 egg
2 T. lemon juice

Mix ingredients thoroughly and drop a teaspoonful of the mixture into confectioner's sugar. Drop onto an ungreased cookie sheet. Bake at 350° for 10 minutes. Cookies will be gooey.

PUMPKIN PATCH FUN

Not to steal anything from Linus, but a pumpkin patch would be a great place for a moon walk. Or a cornfield or haystack. Just be sure to add a cozy blanket to your picnic pack. Find an inviting spot to enjoy some hot chocolate and this homemade caramel corn. Your daughter will be asking for it. And it's so easy to make, she can make it with you.

HOMEMADE CARAMEL CORN

When my kids were tweens, they helped me make this. I did the microwave cooking and they did the shaking.

1 cup unpopped popping corn
1 cup brown sugar
½ cup butter
¼ cup corn syrup
½ tsp. vanilla
½ tsp. salt
½ tsp. baking soda

Pop and salt corn. Put it in a large brown grocery bag. Combine sugar, butter, corn syrup, salt, and vanilla. Microwave on high for 4 minutes. Stir after each minute. Microwave on high for 2 minutes. Add baking soda. Pour over popcorn in the large bag. Nuke for 1.5 minutes in the bag. Shake thoroughly. Nuke for 1 minute in the bag. Shake thoroughly. Pour popcorn on a cookie sheet, bake at 250 for 15 minutes, stir, and bake for another 15 minutes. Cool before serving.

WINTER WONDERLAND

Starting these conversations during the cold winter months? No worries. The only thing better than a moonlit beach is a moonlit fresh snowfall. Try to watch for a really beautiful night. The moon will illuminate the snow-covered fields, making your object lesson all the more powerful. You obviously won't take your snack outside to enjoy—it'll be too cold. But you can find a cozy fireplace to sit by when you get back to enjoy this hot vanilla milk, perhaps with some pretzels or apple slices.

HOT VANILLA MILK

1 cup 2 percent milk
2 tsp. sugar
2 tsp. vanilla extract
1 tsp. ground cinnamon
whipped topping or marshmallows (optional)

Pour the milk into a microwave-safe mug. Stir together the cinnamon and sugar, then stir into the milk. (Mixing the cinnamon and sugar first will help to keep it from floating on top of the milk.) Stir in the vanilla. Heat in microwave for 1 minute and 40 seconds (or longer for a warmer drink). Stir before drinking. Top with whipped topping and marshmallows if you desire.

5

CONVERSATION TWO

YOUR BODY, ITS PRACTICE

When I saw our daughter for the first time, I knew she was born with her Grammy's sweet, button nose. I gently placed my thumb in the curve of it and then planted my first kiss on my just-minutes old daughter right there. Oh, how I love her little nose.

"Who do I look like?"

Both of my girls have asked that question.

Answering the daughter born of my womb was easy. She has her dad's big, steel-blue eyes and full lips. The shape of her face came from me as did the shape of her body. She walks like me. And talks like Bob.

Finding answers to this question has been more difficult and sometimes painful for the daughter born of my heart. We have no record of her birth parents. Not even a photo or name. We don't often discuss this question, but it is there in her heart. Maybe you have an adopted treasure and understand this deep wound. I've made a point of declaring how we are alike. My sweet adopted girl doesn't like to watch a movie a second time. Neither do I. She prefers to get her work done early in the day rather than wait. So do I.

We all long to be like someone.
To belong.
And there's a reason for it.

> Your daughter's primary practice is to
> look like God, and she does that best
> by embracing her role as a girl!

God never wants us to forget that ultimately, we look like him. The next conversation you need to have with your daughter sits solidly on the truth that her primary *purpose* is to glorify God. Since that means she must make him known and visible, her primary *practice* will be to look like him.

Have you ever struggled with your role as a woman? Maybe you've hit a very man-made glass ceiling. (I firmly believe these are not crafted by God. In Scripture, He has suggested some distinctions of roles for men and women, highlighted some of their inherent strengths, and even outlined some preferences, but he designed us to be co-regents together in caring for his world.) Perhaps you, like me, have had a hard time with the idea of biblical submission in marriage. My friend and former True Girl lead teacher Suzy Weibel grew up with incredible athletic ability. She could compete with the best of the boys but sometimes wasn't invited to the game. (She married a guy who always invites her.)

The topic of gender roles can be a difficult thing.

And yet God created our biological sex with intended purpose and guidelines to follow, and these help us to live out our purpose to glorify and enjoy him. Therefore, it's critical to truthfully and honestly answer our children's questions about gender.

Lindsay Leigh Bentley was a tomboy from the get-go, and her parents encouraged her. But they didn't label her. Today she's a beautiful, long-haired, feminine, blonde mother. She's happily married to a guy who is content to do all the clothes shopping and let Lindsay change the oil in the car.

Lindsay's oldest son likes pink. About that, this gutsy blogger writes, "Henry can like pink as much as I like tearing up concrete without it defining our gender."[10]

What *does* define gender?

That's the question we'll answer during today's date.

If this makes you nervous, don't let it—unless you decide not to begin addressing this issue. That would be like ignoring the elephant in our culture's living room. And rest assured, the content you'll be sharing with your daughter isn't going to include anything that would make you uncomfortable. When it comes to gender, we don't need to hyper-focus on the counterfeits. We just need to get acquainted with God's original design.

In fact, just to give you confidence about how easy this is going to be, how about I outline a conversation for you right here.

Mom: On our last date, we learned that our primary purpose is to glorify God. We went for a walk on a moonlit night and learned that the moon has no light of its own. It's simply reflecting the sun, reminding us that the sun exists. That's what it means to glorify God—to remind others that he exists.

On this date, we're going to dive a little deeper. If our primary purpose is to glorify God, our primary practice—that is, the way we apply our purpose to everyday living—must be to look like him so we can represent him. I believe we do that best in the roles of maleness and femaleness—as boys and girls or men and women. Let me explain.

Today our Bible verse is Genesis 1:27:

So God created man in his own image,
in the image of God he created him;
male and female he created them.

An image is a picture of something. So the image of God is a picture of God. In this case, we are the image, so we're like statues! What does this verse specifically say makes us look like the image of God?

Daughter: (Answer: being male and female.)

Mom: So being a girl is a big deal! (And so is being a boy.) It's the *one* thing God points out that makes us look like him. There are lots of things that make us God-like. Our intellect. Our creativity. But God mentions only our gender, or sex, in Genesis when he chooses to make us male and female. Any ideas why he chose two very different genders to help us look like him?

Daughter: (This one is difficult, but let her explore it. The answer you want her to arrive at is that God is three in one. And God created male and female to be distinctly different and yet capable of unity through marriage. In this way, we are like God.)

Mom: Because God is three in one. God the Father. God the Son. God the Holy Spirit. Each distinctly different, but yet one. So God created male and female to be distinctly different and yet capable of being unified through marriage. Of course, it's not a greater honor to be a boy or a greater honor to be a girl. Girls can express their womanhood in lots of different ways. Some like ball games. Others like tea parties. The important thing is that we celebrate being made in the image of God as girls. Let me read a little bit of the Bible to you. This is from Psalm 139:13-14. King David is writing to God.

You formed my inward parts;
  you knitted me together in my mother's womb.
I praise you, for I am fearfully and
  wonderfully made.
Wonderful are your works;
  my soul knows it very well.

According to this verse, who decided you and I would be girls?

Daughter: (Answer: God did.)

Mom: What an honor that God chose for us to be girls! And some to be boys! Let's embrace it. If we celebrate our womanhood, we are saying to God, "I'm happy to look like you. I'm happy to be an image bearer as a girl."

Before you dive into this conversation, won't you take time right now to present your daughter's womanhood to the God who chose it? Ask him to plant in her an understanding of what it means to be a woman and why he chose it for her. Ask him to help her understand the concept of being his image bearer.

PLANNING CONVERSATION TWO

A GIRLS' NIGHT OUT

Subject: image bearing

Setting options: A creperie, teahouse, bakery, or any place chick food is sold. Or a baseball clubhouse, sports bar, or pizza place. Use your daughter's personality to pick the kind of place where you'll host your girls' night out.

Recommendation: Do this with a group of women. Ideally, women and their daughters who are using this book. Since each woman will be unique in her expression of femininity, your daughter will be able to avoid getting stuck in stereotypes while still embracing her role as a woman.

Materials you'll need:

- Each adult or young adult woman attending should bring a photo (from Pinterest, or Instagram, or taken by herself) that represents what it means to be a woman and why she loves it. (Ideas: This can be a picture of a tomboy playing softball, and the woman who shares it can say that she loves being a woman who gets to play sports. Or it can be a picture of a woman with a baby, and the woman who shares it can say she loves that women get to give birth and care for babies. You get the idea. Let it reflect the woman. The photos will be as diverse as your guest list.)

- this book

Select your destination and invite your guests. Make sure you tell them to bring a photo that reflects their style of womanhood.

Once you are at the restaurant, begin by enjoying a meal together. Have your conversation after the meal is cleaned up or during dessert. You have one specific task, and it's very easy. Each woman will show the group her photo, share her thoughts on womanhood, and present her photo to your daughter. (More ideas: This can be a picture of a little girl playing dress-up, and the woman who shares it can say that she still loves to dress up and express her beauty. Or it can be a picture of a woman working, and the woman who shares it can say how she loves that God invites women to work hard.)

Wrap up this sharing time by presenting your own photo and the conversational teaching in this chapter. If you are using *It's Great to Be a Girl*, do meditation 2 together or assign it as homework. If you do not have that book, you can discuss these things.

1. Read Genesis 1:27 and talk about the word God uses to describe maleness and femaleness. (Answer: "image" or "statue.") What does it mean that we are the image or statue of God? (Answer: He wants others to see him, so we must look like him in some way.)

2. List some ways that boys and girls are very different. (Answer: body parts, physical strength, interests…) Review why God would have us be so very different but still be capable of using us to look like him. (Answer: God the Father, God the Son, and God the Holy Spirit are distinctively different and yet unified as one. Since man and woman are different but can become united in marriage, we are a picture of God.)

3. Read Ephesians 5:31-32. Talk about how maleness and femaleness comes together to be one. (Answer: marriage.)

GIRLS' NIGHT OUT IDEAS AND RECIPES

BUDGET CRUNCHER

A girls' night out at someone's home can be an inexpensive and fun way to facilitate this conversation. Each woman can bring one dish to share. You and your daughter should either make your food together before you go or make separate dishes. Let her be a part of the food fun! Here are some themes that could make food prep really fun as well as a few recipes. All of these recipes are super easy to make. Your daughter could do them with little help from you.

WINTERY SOUP AND SALAD NIGHT

Assign everyone either soup or salad and let the host simply prepare her home and do the serving.

EASY CHEESY SOUP

This can be prepared and ready to serve in about 20 minutes. Your daughter can make it with just a little supervision. Be sure to teach her cooktop safety skills before you turn her loose. I've served this one for years to rave reviews! Everyone always asks for my recipe, but I refuse to share it, saying it's much too complicated. Well, now the secret is out!

1 bag Ore-Ida Potatoes O'Brien
(includes potatoes, onions, and peppers)
6 cups water
1 can cream of chicken soup
1 lb. Velveeta cheese, cubed
1 dash Worcestershire sauce
salt and pepper to taste

Put water, cream of chicken soup, and potato mix into a large pot. Bring to boil and cook until the potatoes are soft. Turn down to medium heat and stir in the cubed cheese. Finish off with the remaining ingredients and serve immediately.

SUMMER FUN PATIO PARTY

Assign everyone a fun summer food to add to the host's favorite grilled dish.

ORANGE FROST DRINKS (LACTOSE FREE)

What's a patio party without really fun drinks? Mix this up for some delicious lactose-free fun.

1¼ cups Cool Whip
1 can frozen orange juice concentrate
1 can water
1½ cups crushed ice

Place all ingredients in a blender for one minute until the mixture is smooth. Pour into fun glasses or cups and top it off with a straw and a slice of orange.

FALL HARVEST PARTY

Assign everyone fun fall-themed food to bring, such as corn on the cob or green beans and potatoes cooked in ham juice (a favorite of our family in harvest season).

EASY APPLE CRISP (FAST AND MICROWAVED)

Ya gotta have apples in the fall, and this fun recipe is easy to make.

6 Granny Smith apples, sliced and peeled
8 graham crackers
¾ cup brown sugar
½ cup oatmeal
½ cup flour
1 tsp. cinnamon
½ tsp. allspice or nutmeg
½ cup melted butter

Fill a pie pan ¾ full of apples. Finely chop graham crackers and stir together with other dry ingredients. Add butter and mix well. Spoon moist mixture over apple slices. Microwave on high for 12–15 minutes. Cool slightly and serve with Cool Whip or ice cream.

SPRING BRUNCH

Assign everyone yummy brunch food to bring.

PIÑA COLADA FRUIT DIP

Every spring brunch needs a fun fruit dish. Cut up your favorite fruits and put them on a platter with this tasty dip in the center.

1 8-oz. can crushed pineapple
½ cup milk
½ cup sour cream
1 pkg. instant coconut pudding

Mix all ingredients together and serve chilled.

YOGURT AND GRANOLA FRUIT PARFAITS

Everyone will think they are eating dessert, not healthy yogurt!

1 cup granola
2 cups plain yogurt
1 cup berries
2 T. honey

Layer each pretty parfait or ice cream glass in this order: granola, yogurt, fruit. Drizzle the top with honey. Keep refrigerated until you serve.

6

CONVERSATION THREE

YOUR BODY, GOD'S TEMPLE

M om, when will I be old enough to shave?" asked my daughter. The expression on her face was priceless but unreadable.

Before I tell you what happened next, take a look at these stats from the National Survey of US Women on How and Why They Shave, conducted by the Opinion Research Corporation in March, 2008. The women were asked, "The first time you shaved, did you ask permission or did you sneak it?" Thirty-nine percent probably giggled a bit when they admitted that they'd sneaked it. Another 37 percent said they asked for permission. The rest couldn't remember.[11] So if your daughter is even asking you for permission to shave, give her a hug!

So what did I do? I gave my girl a hug and told her we could talk about it. I added that she could shave whenever she felt ready.

"I already did," she confessed. "Look."

And my precious nine-year-old flashed the smoothest shave mankind has ever seen!

Hygiene isn't easy to discuss biblically simply because there's not a lot about practical cleansing in the Bible. (There's much more on ritual cleansing.) But one thing stands true—our bodies are holy temples for the living God of the universe. Your daughter needs to know this.

Your daughter's body is a temple of the living God—his dwelling place.

If God is living in our bodies, then they should be cared for better than the Taj Mahal.

The Bible does tell us to take care of our bodies, and it gives reasons as well. Before we begin to talk to your daughter about them, let's consider how well we are doing at living out what we're about to teach. Evaluate yourself in each of these three basic body-care issues. (You'll be working on them with your daughter this week, so that may give you a chance to reboot as well!)

Are you drinking an eight-ounce glass of water eight times each day? Paul tells his mentee to quit drinking only water because he was often sick (1 Timothy 5:23). Timothy may have been drinking polluted water. We don't really know, but in the first century, people in the Middle East probably had less access to clean water than folks enjoy today. At any rate, Paul tells Timothy to take care of himself with what he's drinking. Drinking is a big deal. In my case, I need *more* water. Not less.

Did you know that the number one ingredient in your body is water? Your body is 60 percent water. Your brain, 75 percent. And your lungs are 80 percent water. If you don't replenish these vital organs with a daily intake of fresh water, you are more likely to struggle with feeling sluggish and tired. Parts of your body may struggle with acne, allergies, brittle hair, and so on. A lack of water can cause all these and more as the bigger organs hog what little is brought in.

Are you taking good care of your body? In Ephesians 5:28, Paul tells husbands they should love their wives just as they love themselves. He says it in a way that highlights our natural emphasis on caring for ourselves. In other words, it's natural to take better care of ourselves than anyone else possibly would. I try to get eight hours of sleep, eat when I'm hungry, take a really good shower every day, and enjoy a massage whenever I can. Why? As Paul said, "No one hates his own body but feeds and cares for it, just as Christ cares for the church" (verse 29 NLT).

Up to this point, you've probably been the one caring for your daughter's body. Helping her remember to bathe, reminding her when to eat, telling her it's bedtime. Right about now, it's time to become more formal in handing the reins over to her to care for her own body. You'll do that best by example! Do you take good care of yourself?

Are you mindful that your body must be well-cared for because it is God's dwelling place? In 1 Corinthians 6:19, Paul explains the reason why what we do with our bodies matters. "Don't you realize that your body is the temple of the Holy Spirit, who lives in you and was given to you by God?" If the Holy Spirit has taken up residence in our bodies...well, I don't know about you, but I'm going to bring in the best housekeeping service available. I don't want the most important relationship in my life to play out in squalor! This demands, for example, that I think of food as fuel for God's temple, not solely pleasure for my palate. Anything I do with my body should take into consideration how it will make it stronger for the Lord.

--- --- ---

Just as you have to learn to cook or play an instrument, you had to learn skills in order to care for your body. (I know a guy whose parents never told him about deodorant. It wasn't until he got to college and had a roommate that he heard about it and was mortified that he'd been left out on this important Secret. Pun intended!) Even something as simple as that needs to be introduced and taught! So…let's take our girls to school.

This conversation is going to move into the practical territory of body care. As you are running water for the most amazing bubble bath in all of human history, give your daughter a Body Boost gift basket or bag. (Look for ideas for that in the shaded box below.) You can include anything you want, but be sure to have one item for each of the Body Boosts below. The Body Boosts are written straight to your daughter. Read or share the thoughts included in each one with her before you send her into a bubbly bath to soak and enjoy and try some new things. (These Body Boosts were not my idea. Former True Girl lead teacher Suzy Weibel shared them with me. I love them!)

BODY BOOST GIFT BASKET

Create a fun basket for your daughter that includes items she'll use not only in her bubble bath but also on a regular basis from this day forward. Be sure to include what she's ready for but not things she doesn't yet need. For example, a nine-year-old may not need acne medication just yet. Hold off on that and maybe just buy her a simple facial cleanser.

  bubble bath

  body moisturizer

  facial cleanser or acne medication

  deodorant and/or body spray

  razor and shaving cream

  loofah sponge

  water bottle

No need to include hair products because we're headed to the hair salon to learn about hair care in the next date.

BODY BOOST IDEAS

Body Boost 1—Soap

Boys aren't the only ones who get stinky. You'll just have to trust me because we aren't always the best judges of what we smell like. Why is it we love the swimming pool so much and yet we treat taking a bath or shower as if it were the black plague? Let's make sure the smells we are broadcasting to the world cooperate with our desire to have others near us by committing to daily or every-other-day bubble baths or showers. You can do this in the morning or at night if that fits your schedule better, but it's time to get serious about it. (Mom, by the time your daughter's breast buds have appeared, it's a good idea to consider a shower at least every other day. For the next few years, her body is going to make extra smells, so daily is a better bet!)

Body Boost 2—Facial Cleanser

So what causes pimples (or acne)? It's pretty complicated, because God's design of your body is crazy good. We often put lotions on our skin to provide moisture, but in many cases we don't need to do so. The skin is full of pores (or hair follicles) that produce their own oils. The oil-producing glands in your pores are called sebaceous glands. Puberty hormones tell these sebaceous glands to increase production of skin oil, but sometimes the glands work a little overtime, and dead skin cells or bacteria get trapped inside your pores along with too much oil. This produces a pimple.

Two things prevent pimples—keeping your face clean and keeping your hands clean (especially before you cleanse or touch your face). You can really prevent them by starting to wash your face regularly *before* they start to show up!

Once one shows up, it's best to let it run its natural course. It'll most likely be gone within a week. If the pimple does turn white, that means the trapped oils and bacteria are near the surface and can be more safely "popped," though you should never deal with pimples unless your hands are washed and you are able to immediately put an antibacterial wash on the sore. If you can, resist the temptation to "pop" a pimple. Makeup is a great and safe way to cover the redness.

Best way to prevent pimples to begin with? Wash your face every morning and night like clockwork, but there's no need to wash too often or to scrub like crazy. Again, God's design is amazing. A simple wash will remove dead skin cells, which are the main culprits getting trapped in those open pores. If you use a moisturizing cream afterward, be sure it is "non-acnegenic"—a fancy way to say it does not clog your pores. And watch out for those hair sprays and gels! They tend to make acne worse.

Body Boost 3–Deodorant

Time to start using deodorant. There are very few things as offensive to other people's noses as body odor. But I'm willing to bet your own nose has taught you that. You might be one of the lucky few who don't need to wear deodorant every day. Want to hear a simple rule that applies to much of life? Less is more. It can't get much easier than that, can it? Less deodorant. Less perfume. Less offending other people even with your good smells. It can be tempting to put on a lot of something that smells really good. But a lot of perfume…well, it smells really bad.

Body Boost 4–Razor

Eventually you'll most likely want to shave your legs and underneath your arms. This is considered standard hygiene for most Americans, but you might be surprised to know that girls in many other countries do not shave.

Shaving is one of the more difficult hygiene practices to master. No one is good at this one right from the start, which is a bit of a scary thought since we're talking about a sharp object!

There are alternatives to shaving, though none are as quick or as cheap. One alternative is waxing, which is just what it sounds like. Hot wax (not so hot it burns) is applied to the skin, and a strip of paper or cloth is laid on top of it. After a second of warmth, the strip is ripped from the skin, taking the wax and the hair (from the root) with it. *Ouch*! Why wax? The hair stays gone longer. A lot longer. Why not wax? Pain would be a good reason number one, along with the fact that waxing has a tendency to cause pimples. It's also a lot more expensive than a razor and soap.

Some companies also sell "hair removal cream," or depilatories. (Put that word on your vocab list this week.) This is a cream containing chemicals that break down the properties of body hair so it can easily be removed from the site of its follicle. Why use a cream? Cream can't cut you, now can it? But I find more reasons not to use the creams. I'm cautious about using too many chemicals on skin. The cream's hair-removal effects last no longer than shaving. And shaving creams typically have a really nice smell, but these hair removal creams tend to have a foul odor.

Hair can also be lightened rather than removed, though this involves chemicals again, and I still don't like chemicals even though three sentences have come and gone.

A newer technique involves buying a handheld sander and literally using the friction of sandpaper to remove hair. This is an expensive little machine to buy, and you'd need to buy a lot of sandpaper over the years. Hair removed by this method sometimes comes in thicker for some reason, so it seems silly to me. The one good thing we can say about sanding is that it also removes dead skin cells and leaves skin smooth.

Finally, crazy brave people may use little electric shocks to remove hair for long periods of time…enough said. Shocks. No thank you.

By now you're probably starting to realize it really does take a lot of work to keep yourself presentable and healthy through good hygiene. But there's one aspect of hygiene we didn't discuss, and that is a social one. In other words, good hygiene helps us have good relationships with other people because they don't want to avoid us and our bad smells.

Body Boost 5–Water

Did you know that drinking water will make you beautiful? It's true. Of course, it's also important for other reasons. Water helps you digest food and circulate blood, and it even makes it easier to…um… "excrete." But drinking water will also help you have healthier-looking, glowing skin. After all, your skin is an organ made up of cells, and cells are made up of water. They need water to function well. If you don't drink enough water, your skin could become dry and itchy.

There are two ways to care for your body with water. One is to drink it! Lots of it. An eight-ounce glass eight times a day. Having a water bottle with ounces marked on it will help you remember how much to drink.

A second way is to moisturize within two minutes of leaving the bath or shower. This sort of seals the water into your pores so you stay hydrated. Just slather on some good moisturizer.

PLANNING CONVERSATION THREE

A BODY-BOOSTING BUBBLE BATH

Subject: hygiene

Setting options: a Jacuzzi tub at a hotel, Grandma's, or your own house

Materials you'll need:

- Reservations at a hotel, or a resort, or Grandma's. You might also just plan to do this at your own home.

- a Body Boost gift bag or basket full of hygiene products, such as deodorant, shampoo, a razor, and body wash

- this book

For the best results of fantastic Bible study, use *It's Great to Be a Girl*. Do meditation 3 together. If you don't have that book, you can discuss these things.

1. Read 1 Corinthians 3:16-17. What does it call your body? (Answer: a temple.) A temple is a place where God lives, so

that means God's Spirit is living in you. How does that make you feel? (Answers will vary.)

2. Does God's Spirit live in everyone? (Answer: No. He lives in those who have asked Christ to be the Lord of their life. If you or your daughter have not made this decision, read "The ABCs of Becoming a Christian" starting on page 62.)

3. If God is living in us, what does that say about how we should care for our bodies? (Answers will vary: We should clean them, provide nutrition for them, avoid putting harmful substances in them…)

HOME SPA RECIPES

If you're going all homemade and want to make this date extra fun, here are a few spa recipes you can whip up for your date.

OATMEAL-HONEY FACE MASK

1 cup natural yogurt
½ cup oatmeal
2 T. honey
4 cucumber slices (for your eyes)

Mix the first three ingredients. You may like the yogurt to be cool in the summer or room temperature in the winter. The honey makes it a great moisturizing mask, but if you or your daughter have oily skin, skip it and squeeze in the juice of a lime or lemon to create a drying mask.

Once the mask is mixed, put it on your face and lie down. Add the cucumbers to your eyes to depuff. Enjoy the treatment for 10–15 minutes.

Be prepared to giggle and laugh while you're enjoying this, but also use the time to talk to your daughter about the importance of cleansing her face as she moves towards puberty.

Wash the mask off using a washcloth steamed in the microwave. (Make sure it's not too hot before applying.)

TROPICAL BREEZE SPA DRINK

1 sliced lemon
1 sliced lime
1 sliced orange
mint leaves to taste

Add to a glass pitcher of water and let it set for an hour or so. The flavors will create a refreshing and healthy drink to enjoy during your spa treatments.

THE ABCs OF BECOMING A CHRISTIAN

Your body is the temple of the living God once you offer him access. God has given us free will to surrender our lives to him or to be our own god. When we relinquish control, we become a Christian, and the Bible teaches that God's Spirit comes to dwell within us.

What does it mean to be a Christian? Is it going to church? Being raised in a Christian home? Being told you are a Christian? You need to understand this first for yourself and then for your daughter. Believing that going to church, being good, or calling yourself a Christian is your ticket to heaven is very dangerous if you have never actually chosen to follow Jesus Christ in obedience. Jesus himself said he was the only way to heaven. John 14:6 reads, "Jesus said...'I am the way, the truth, and the life. No one comes to the Father except through me.'" Still, many people are confused by things and actions that do not make them Christians any more than talking in a New Zealand accent makes me a Kiwi! Here are the simple ABCs of becoming a Christian.

A—Admit you are a sinner. A person must start with the confession that she has sinned. She must be sorry for her sin and willing to stop. Whether she is reading sexually charged novels, cheating on her taxes, gossiping...all sin separates us from God. Because he is perfect and holy, he cannot be in the presence of uncleansed sin. Romans 3:23 says, "All have sinned and fall short of the glory of God." There's that word again—"glory." We cannot reflect God's image if there is sin in us. And this verse says we're all guilty.

If you know you have sinned, pause to verbally confess your sin to God right now.

B—Believe that Jesus is the Son of God and that his death on the cross was payment for all your sins. You may be familiar with John 3:16. That beloved Bible verse reads, "For God so loved the world, that he gave his only Son, that whoever believes in him should not perish but have eternal life." Someone had to pay the price for our sinfulness. God loved us enough to offer up his Son in our place. It is a selfless and crazy love that God lavishes on us. He sacrificed his only Son so we can live with him. He desires fellowship with you so earnestly that he has given his all.

If you believe Jesus is God's Son, pause to say that to him out loud.

C—Confess your faith in Jesus out loud to God and to others. Romans 10:9-10 says, "If you confess with your mouth that Jesus is Lord and believe in your heart that God raised him from the dead, you will be saved." Salvation requires your mouth! You must tell God and other people that Jesus is the Lord of your life.

If you want Jesus to be the Lord of your life, begin by pausing to ask him verbally right now. Then pick up the phone and tell someone! Hop on social media and tell me. I'd so love to know that you prayed this prayer and have become my sister in Jesus today. Welcome to the family!

Still uncertain? Does that seem too simple? Well, even the most brilliant of minds brought the Christian faith down to simple concepts. Blaise Pascal, a Christian philosopher and a brilliant physicist and mathematician, offered what has come to be known as "Pascal's wager." He basically said that deciding whether to believe in Christ is like placing a bet because it requires faith. He said that believing is ultimately the smarter choice. If we bet on Christ being God's Son who died for our sins and we're wrong, we end up losing some finite earthly pleasures (gluttony, materialism, promiscuity, and so on). But if we bet against him and we're wrong, we end up losing infinite goodness (heaven in place of hell).

Smart man, that Pascal. Something to consider if you're still unsure of what you believe. As for me, I'm not a gambler, but I'm putting it all on Jesus!

7

CONVERSATION FOUR

YOUR HAIR, A CROWN

just cut off about six inches of my hair.

I don't like it. It's way too short.

But I'm not upset, and I didn't shed a single tear over it. The fact is, it'll be a lot healthier now. And funny thing about hair—it grows.

I've come a long way, baby.

When I was in middle school, my mom gave me my first at-home perm. Apparently, a few of the rollers on the crown of my head were a tad tight. And the solution was on a bit too long. I got another kind of haircut altogether. My shoulder-length, chemically induced curls were literally topped off with a nice short shock of one-inch, stick-straight hair standing at attention like a soldier where the chemicals had given me a hack job.

I cried, much the same way my daughter did when she decided to go short in middle school. She came home with tears flowing down her cheeks.

That's what we do in middle school. We cry about the way that we look.

Okay, the truth is that I've been a bit too self-conscious in my adult years, even if I haven't cried. Not this time. Not this haircut. But sometimes.

Are you guilty?

Hair that is well cared for can be beautiful. And yet the apostle Paul asks us why. "If a woman has long hair, is it her glory?"

Well, is it?

Nope. If you've been paying attention to our lessons, you have been well reminded that our entire being is for his glory. Nothing is to bring *us* glory. It's all for him! (More on that verse in a moment.)

Everything from the tip of our toes to the top of our head is for his glory, including our hair.

Our hair is part of the temple of God. In fact, Proverbs says that gray hair is a crown of glory! I'll confess that I'm not going gray without a bit of a fight. My battle tools are frequent highlights and low-lights!

Hair is just fun! I don't think we need to get that spiritual and deep about the fact that I like mine long and my best girl Suzy likes hers cropped and spiked. This is an area where you and I can have our own preferences, and they may be very unlike our daughters'. When your sweet baby girl comes to you and wants to shave one side of her head and dye the other side purple, what will you say?

Mom, this is a perfect time for you and me to talk about legalism. Because, oh, I desire for you to be a mom who shuns legalism. Rules without relationship lead to rebellion. I've said many times that sometimes we need to bend our preferences—but not God's mandates!—in order to let our children face giants God has assigned to them. Having unbending rules is far easier, but Mom, grace is messy! Let's use hairstyles as an example as we delve into the topic of legalism. Consider 1 Corinthians 11:4-16 (NLT).

> A man dishonors his head if he covers his head while praying or prophesying. But a woman dishonors her head if she

prays or prophesies without a covering on her head, for this is the same as shaving her head. Yes, if she refuses to wear a head covering, she should cut off all her hair! But since it is shameful for a woman to have her hair cut or her head shaved, she should wear a covering.

A man should not wear anything on his head when worshiping, for man is made in God's image and reflects God's glory. And woman reflects man's glory. For the first man didn't come from woman, but the first woman came from man. And man was not made for woman, but woman was made for man. For this reason, and because the angels are watching, a woman should wear a covering on her head to show she is under authority.

But among the Lord's people, women are not independent of men, and men are not independent of women. For although the first woman came from man, every other man was born from a woman, and everything comes from God.

Judge for yourselves. Is it right for a woman to pray to God in public without covering her head? Isn't it obvious that it's disgraceful for a man to have long hair? And isn't long hair a woman's pride and joy? For it has been given to her as a covering. But if anyone wants to argue about this, I simply say that we have no other custom than this, and neither do God's other churches.

In my younger years, this passage was used legalistically in some church circles. It was written to a church in the Middle East, where—to this day—covering your head is considered a way to show respect to those who are in authority over you. The point was that women (and men) showed respect and submission to God, not that they had their hair covered. The church felt that it was really important for women to cover their heads because God was the one we show submission to—not a boss or family member, but the *God of the universe*! However, men and women were fighting about it because it also symbolized that man was created first and was the "head" of the woman.

While this is true, some men weren't kind about how they responded to women. And some women were so upset about this that they shaved their heads to show that no one was in charge of them! (Can you say, "rebellious"?) In order to control the rebels, the people wanted Paul to make a hard-and-fast rule that all women should always have long hair and always cover their heads when they prayed. (Can you say, "legalism"?) Paul's answer is clear in The Message:

> *Don't you agree there is something naturally powerful in the symbolism—a woman, her beautiful hair reminiscent of angels, praying in adoration; a man, his head bared in reverence, praying in submission? I hope you're not going to be argumentative about this. All God's churches see it this way; I don't want you standing out as an exception* (1 Corinthians 11:13-16).

Basically Paul is saying, stop fighting about *how* to show respect to God and each other, and just do it! He refused to take sides with a legalistic rule about hair, but he also didn't let them off the hook. They needed to respect God with the right heart!

Let's answer a few questions about the practice of cutting and coloring our hair from a biblical perspective, because this is a great place for us moms to cool the jets, so to speak, as we teach our daughters.

Is it okay to cut your hair? Okay, you're probably not struggling with this one, but let's explore it. Some use 1 Corinthians 1:15 to say that we cannot cut our hair, but that's not really true. Paul writes, "*If* a woman has long hair…" The word "if" is implying that it is not a must, but a maybe. A woman might have long hair. She might not. Not everyone has the good fortune of thick, full hair. And some that do, wish theirs could be straight and light. Nothing is wrong with cutting your hair into a style that suits your face and figure and makes you feel confident. Our hair is part of our body, so it should be groomed and cared for as part of God's temple. Need a haircut? I say, "Snip, snip!"

Is it okay to color your hair? (Let's go a step further: Is it okay to color your hair blue?) The Bible doesn't give us instructions on this, but it does say that gray hair is a crown. Some use the passage to declare that we must never color our hair. You may feel comfortable letting the gray come naturally. Go for it, and let it be your crown. But nowhere does the Bible prohibit hair color. If dying your hair makes you look better and you enjoy the results, grab a box and go for it! (Just remember that desire when your daughter comes to you asking for a trending color treatment that seems odd to you!)

When I began leading retreats for teen girls, I met a girl with bright pink, spiked, short hair. I confess—I judged her before I knew her, expecting her to be a challenge. Instead, I found her to be a great lover of Jesus, and her expressive hair and personality opened the hearts of other girls to love Jesus too. I remember telling myself that if my girls wanted to color their hair pink or purple or anything else, I'd be agreeable as long as their hearts were as lovely as this girl's was.

When one of my girls was in fourth grade, she asked if she could color her hair to celebrate staying home for a year of homeschooling. Without hesitation, I said yes, and she enjoyed cotton-candy pink highlights that year!

Do what you like with your hair, but be sure that you're blessing the Lord in your heart as you do it!

There are two goals during this conversation challenge. The first is for her to see that everything about her glorifies God—even her hair. (And we have some pretty amazing verses to prove that God thinks about her hair too!) Your second goal is for your daughter to start thinking about hair care and learning to do it on her own. A lot of this conversation is going to be practical—and fun!

Due to the fact that hair care differs tremendously based on the kind of hair you have, I won't be giving specific hair-care advice in these pages. Instead, I'll mention the topics to cover. You can either develop this conversation on your own or ask a stylist to cover these topics with your daughter if you have this conversation during a salon appointment. (Good idea, huh?)

Washing. Discuss how often this should be done, what types of shampoo and conditioner to use, and any specific before or after care depending on hair type. (For example, someone with dry, curly hair may have to learn how to detangle it before or after a shampoo.)

Drying. Discuss the healthiest way to dry hair (air drying) and why it is sometimes appropriate to dry it with a blow dryer (because it makes it look more finished and clean). Offer blow-drying tips for her hair type.

Cutting. Based on hair type and finances, how often should your daughter plan to have her hair cut? What are the benefits of cutting it?

Styling. Give her some fun ideas of how to style her hair. Here are some snapshots from other True Girls and brief instructions on how to get each look.

1. Alayna • Illusion Mermaid Braid with a twist: Do a French fishtail braid in the center of the back of your head. Complete about four strands, divide the hair in half, and do two fishtail braids. Tuck the ends under and secure at the base of your neck under the braid with bobby pins.

2. Mya • Waterfall Braid: Similar to a French braid, but instead of picking up a new piece of hair with each "braid," allow the piece to fall and choose an entirely new piece to incorporate into the braid.

3. ZaanuYa • Pom-Poms: Part your hair down the center from forehead to nape of your neck. Gather each part tightly with a ponytail holder directly above each ear. (From left to right: Sorochi, Maruchechi, and ZaanuYa.)

4. Carolina • Low Side Ponytail Pinwheel: A handmade over-the-top embellished headband with hair in a low side ponytail.

PLANNING CONVERSATION FOUR

A NEW "DO"

Subject: hair care

Setting options: a salon or at-home salon experience

Materials you'll need:

- An appointment at a salon or a creative and fun at-home salon experience, in which case you'll need shampoos, towels, blow dryer, rollers, hairpins, and so on. If you do the at-home salon, be sure to check out the snapshots of some of my favorite tween girls on page 70.

- this book

I suggest that you and your daughter both get treated to a new "do" during this conversation. Doing is the best way to learn. Find the best little salon in town or create one right in your own home. Make reservations for a haircut, color, or style! Use this activity to bring attention to her hair and discuss the fact that even her hair can glorify God.

For the best results during the conversation, use *It's Great to Be a Girl*. Do meditation 4 together. If you do not have that book, you can discuss these things.

1. Read 1 Corinthians 11:15. Does God say our hair is for our glory? (Answer: No. It is just a covering!) Since we know our body's purpose is to glorify God, what does that say about our hair? (Answer: It can and should glorify God too.)

2. If being distinctly female is a part of glorifying God (as we saw in earlier conversations), what are some ways your hair can help your body glorify God? (Answers will vary but could include these: It should look feminine so I can be distinctly female. I can be clean and well-groomed so I am set apart. When I select a style or color, my intention should not be to glorify myself.)

3. Did you know that God pays such close attention to you that even your hairs are numbered? How many do you think you have? (Let her guess. We each have between 90,000 and 150,000 hairs on our head.)

8

CONVERSATION FIVE

FOOD, YOUR FUEL

When one of my girls was in elementary school, she had a lot of tummy problems. She just never really felt well. Ever. She was often a bit grumpy and difficult to manage when she was not feeling well. Her mood seemed to be directly linked to her food, but I couldn't figure it out. I just knew something was very wrong.

After many visits to many doctors, we still could not get an accurate diagnosis.

Finally, I prayed.

It's interesting how we moms get bold when we get on our knees! I went back to my general practitioner and said, "I'm tired of traveling hours to get one test done at a time while my daughter continues to suffer. We're treating her presumptively, and nothing is working. Can't you order a bunch of tests to be done in one day so we can figure this out? She's been sick for two years!"

Without even a question, he said yes, and we headed straight to the hospital for a full day of tests.

I knew when we'd found it. I saw it on the face of the nurse. My girl's breath test for lactose intolerance was through the roof and then some. The nurse had never seen a reading like this before. No more dairy for my sweet daughter.

Within weeks she was compliant, sweet, fun, and feeling great!

— — —

Does your eating plan require an area of discipline? Maybe your body, like mine, doesn't like wheat very much (more on that in a moment). Maybe, like my daughter, you can't drink milk. Or maybe you just know in your heart that living on Doritos and pizza isn't God's best plan for you, but you continually find yourself devouring them in front of the television. Confess any areas of weakness to God and pray, "Lord, help me to remember that you've given us food to act as fuel."

During this conversation you will begin to establish the foundation upon which you can help your daughter build healthy eating habits. I'm going to try to get one thing into all our heads—including my own:

Food is fuel, not entertainment.

So often we use food to curb boredom, not hunger. We plan our social gatherings around food. People in the Bible did that too, but fettuccine Alfredo, garlic bread, and cheesecake were not on the menu at the last supper. Until more recently, people were eating the food God created for them more often than they were indulging in synthetics. Besides, special meals in the Bible were less common and lots of hard work to bring together, not regular occurrences. There was a rareness and rhythm to feasting. Today, we live in a society that makes feasting an almost daily activity. If we're not careful, special meals begin losing their unique quality, and we start gaining a few extra pounds each month.

In our Western culture, we really do think of food as entertainment, not fuel. I've been reminded of this while writing this book. We are remodeling our kitchen because the old farmhouse we bought had what I'm sure was the very first microwave ever invented and an oven with wires sticking out the sides! Currently, my refrigerator is outside, my grill is in an odd spot outside the house, and my microwave is in the bedroom. This comprises my current kitchen. Food is super simple during these weeks—mostly a piece of grilled meat and a salad that I can throw together in the laundry room. It's fuel, but it's not entertaining in the slightest bit.

Yesterday I declared myself "mentally hungry." I so badly wanted to eat something fancy and fun! And I do think our Western culture feeds this fascination. In many countries where I've worked, I haven't seen the tantalizing billboards for steaks that I see here—the ones that I seem to *hear* sizzling when I'm driving down the highway. (For the record, I call those billboards "food porn.")

Houston, we have a problem!

Childhood obesity in the United States has more than doubled among tweens and quadrupled among teens since you and I were kids. Classified as excessive body fat, it is highly impacted by genetic factors, but even those prone to carry extra weight can control it by eating healthy meals. In this country, about 18.4 percent of kids aged 6 to 11 are obese. But my real concern is that the risk gets higher for your daughter in just a few years as she approaches her teens. Fully 20.5 percent of 12- to 19-year-olds are overweight. This places them on a conveyor belt for heart disease, type 2 diabetes, stroke, several types of cancer, and osteoarthritis. Those things won't impact her until she's much older, but extra weight causes other, more immediate problems. Right away you might see her struggling with sleeping, bone or joint pain, social challenges, and poor self-esteem.[12] No mom wants to sign her kid up for that, but that's what we could be doing when we serve up simple carbs and brownies in the absence of broccoli and peas.

Of course, sometimes our daughters aren't eating enough!

Not a large percentage of girls will succumb to eating disorders, but the effects are so high-risk that every mother needs to be aware of what to watch for, and when. Anorexia—excessive dieting or not eating at all—affects only about 1 percent of young women. But it's among the most difficult of all psychiatric disorders to treat. And while bulimia—bingeing and purging—commonly starts in high school or college, in girls who may be demonstrating some level of depression, anorexia often manifests in those *tweens* who are among the brightest students and highest achievers. This is nothing to mess with, and what your 8- to 12-year-old is exposed to can limit the risk…or increase it.[13]

How can you know if your daughter is struggling with anorexia (withholding food) or bulimia (forcing herself to throw up after she eats)? Watch for these signs and see your doctor if you are concerned.

- refusal to eat
- fear of gaining weight
- negative self-image
- excessive exercise
- flat mood or lack of emotion
- irritability
- obsession over food touching other food on her plate

Let's be proactive with food and introduce healthy fueling skills to our daughters. Let's not let the world's overeating habits and dangerous lies about body image devour our daughters.

— — —

Can we talk about you and me for a moment? Are you and I being good stewards of our bodies when it comes to food? I know I'm guilty of a big fail in this area. (More on how that's impacted me in a moment.)

Obesity is currently under investigation as a potential link to depression and mood disorders. In a 28-year study of 58,000 overweight individuals, more than 50 percent of them struggled with depression. Researchers also found a significant negative impact on memory and cognitive function (think: Alzheimers and dementia) as well as respiratory and musculoskeletal disorders (think: asthma and arthritis). And women face a special risk—we are more likely to struggle with infertility if we have a BMI above 24. (Of course, women with a BMI under 20 are also more likely to struggle with infertility. There is such a thing as being too thin. I'm not advocating for excessive exercise or dieting, but for healthy living!)[14]

My greatest concern is not health for the sake of health. Our bodies are temples of the living God. We should be taking better care of them so we can honor and serve the one who lives in us.

Let me share a little of my own struggle with you and add the warning that indulging in too many empty calories doesn't always look like fat. I carry a few extra pounds and occasionally sport a muffin top, but I'm not that big. Still, some people who are bigger than me are probably healthier than me. The bottom line is not what the scale says, but what your body is trying to tell you. My body was talking to me through stomach and respiratory problems.

After a lifelong struggle with what I'd call nervous stomach, I decided to have it checked out. The doctor prescribed medication to control the symptoms and asserted that nothing could be done.

A few years later, I had a very serious bout with asthma. It was so bad that when recording new video curriculum for my first book *And the Bride Wore White*, I had to be on heavy oral steroids just to speak without coughing. After a few weeks, the doctor added nasal steroids, and I had to mist into my lungs with an inhaler. Girl, I was 'roided up! Again, the doctor told me that though I would be able to get on top of the symptoms, there was no foolproof cure for my lungs.

I was not able to speak to an audience before using the inhalers. If I tried, I would go into an uncontrollable coughing fit on stage.

Soon the side effects of the all the meds were killing me—headaches, weight gain, terrible muscle pain, sleeplessness, and much more.

"I surely can't be meant to live like this," I prayed. "Lord, help me."

A week or so later, I was at Brooklyn Tabernacle for a meeting and decided to stay for the prayer service. I so wanted to enjoy the wonderful worship I knew was coming in just a half an hour, so I decided to pop a pain pill. But then, the Holy Spirit clearly chastised me. It was as if he said in the quiet of my mind, "Dannah, you are in a house of healing. Why would you turn to Advil?"

I strapped on my humility and headed to the prayer altar, where a lovely lady who I think was named Mary listened to my story and then prayed with gentle authority. I remember one sentence as if it were moments ago: "Lord, heal Dannah's lungs to the measure with which she uses them to praise you." What a marching order she gave me! I headed back to my seat and worshipped my lungs silly.

I left that service feeling totally healed. No headache. No coughing. My body didn't even ache as it had earlier. And I had worshipped wholeheartedly, using my lungs without the inhaler! This had been impossible before.

The next morning, I woke up feeling sick again. That's when God prompted me to begin treating my stomach and lung illnesses differently. I began researching and learned that both my "nervous stomach" and my asthma were provoked by simple carbs, especially products made with bleached, white wheat. I also learned that asthma, although terribly difficult to understand, may be an autoimmune disorder in which excessive mucus is treated as an invader and attacked, impacting the lungs negatively. The mucus is worsened by dairy products. This was very bad news for this carb-loving, ice-cream-addicted girl.

I have been known to order a pizza and down it all on my own. Or to pick up a carton of ice cream for a small family function and finish it off within a day with little help. My evening boredom is often curbed by a box of Kraft macaroni and cheese followed by an Eggo with copious amounts of butter and confectioner's sugar. (I did *that* last night!) In short, though I do not look to be terribly overweight, my body was sending me its own Morse-code-like message: "Back away from the carbs. I repeat, back away from the carbs!"

I do not recommend that you do what I did next, and I plead with you to check with your doctor before even considering following my example. But I stopped all my meds cold-turkey.

I also started a new, healthier, veggie-based eating plan, and I signed up for anointing and prayer at my home church. (See James 5:14 if being anointed with oil for healing is a new concept to you. It is a basic instruction for the church that is often overlooked.)

The first week, with no meds and healthier eating only, was touch and go. I was still coughing a lot. But then the elders of my church prayed for me and anointed me with oil as the Bible instructs. Since then, I've had my asthma under control. (I have found that if I eat wheat or simple carbs, I'm prone to some stomach cramping almost immediately. But I've decided an occasional indulgence of my favorite Faccia Luna pizza is totally worth it!)

And the best news is that I'm happier. I didn't realize how my mood was affected by all that unhealthy (but undeniably delicious) food. A pizza is without question an anvil that my lack of willpower ties to my attitude, pulling it down to the deepest, darkest murkiness of moods. Being carb-free makes me happier, more motivated, and more energetic.

God heals. And sometimes he uses food—and discipline— to do it.

The moral of the story: I was cooperating with the enemy of my body and soul in indulging in excessive empty carbs and sugars. This was prohibiting me from serving the Lord onstage and probably slowing me down in all the administrative and writing work he assigns to me. But since I've been using food as fuel rather than entertainment, I've become a more effective temple that can serve the God who dwells within me.

You undoubtedly have your own story. Most of us do. We overeat. Or we don't eat enough. We may even contribute to malnourishment by excessive exercise. Oh, I plead with you to consider how your eating habits will impact your daughter as she sees and learns from your daily living.

Here's a sample conversation for you to consider using as you teach her that food is fuel!

Mom: Just like our car requires gasoline to run, our bodies require fuel to run. What would happen if I never put gasoline into our car?

Daughter: It wouldn't work.

Mom: Your body is just like that. Have you ever felt drained of energy because you didn't get to eat? And have you ever eaten something and felt energized?

Daughter: (Answers will vary.)

Mom: Food is the fuel of your body. When you come to the dinner table each night, it's like driving up to the gas pump for fuel. Did you know there is more than one kind of gas for cars? Poor-quality or low-octane fuel will make my car clang and bang and stop. There's also diesel fuel, and my car won't work with that kind. Our bodies prefer a certain kind of fuel too. We have to be careful about what we put into our bodies. Can you guess which kinds of food are good fuel?

Daughter: (Answers will vary, but lead her to these: vegetables, meats, fruits, nuts...anything natural that God created to eat.)

Mom: Let's read Genesis 1:29 and see what God said is good fuel for our body. It says, "God said, 'Behold, I have given you every plant yielding seed that is on the face of all the earth, and every tree with seed in its fruit. You shall have them for food." When God first created the earth and told Adam and Eve what to eat, what did he include on the list?

Daughter: (Answer: vegetables, fruits, and seeds.)

Mom: That's right. God created us to be able to eat veggies, fruits, and seeds. What isn't on the list that we eat?

Daughter: (Answers will vary: meat, cake, bread...)

Mom: You're right! Do you know when mankind first started to eat meat? After Noah's flood (Genesis 9:4). There weren't many trees, vegetables, or seeds, so God allowed humans to begin to eat meat. But that wasn't his best plan. It was an allowance with one restriction—Noah and his family could eat the meat but were not to drink the blood. There are lots of things God lets us eat as allowances, but he designed our bodies to be fueled by vegetables, fruits, and seeds. Tell me, how does all of this sound to you? Is it new? Strange? Familiar?

Daughter: (Answers will vary.)

Mom: I'd like to see us try to do a little bit better in eating the fuel of vegetables, fruits, and seeds because that's what God had in mind when he first created human bodies. Let's start right now.

PLANNING CONVERSATION FIVE

SALAD AND SMOOTHIE MAKING 101

Subject: food as fuel

Setting options: a kitchen

Materials you'll need:

- grocery items for your favorite smoothie and salad recipes (see recipes provided in this chapter or use your own)

- this book

Have this conversation while you are in the kitchen preparing your smoothies and salads and enjoying your creations. This conversation is rather simple and can be modified based on the information in this chapter that may be helpful to your daughter and your family's nutritional protocol. Your daughter might enjoy helping you decide what to make and going shopping with you.

For the best conversation, use *It's Great to Be a Girl*. Do meditation 5 together. If you do not have that book, you can discuss these things. It is mostly review today, but since this may be a new paradigm, we should make sure your daughter processed it all carefully, including the fact that eating meat, cake, candy, and the like is not sinful or wrong. It's just not what fuels her best.

1. Read Genesis 1:29. What did God originally plan for us to eat? (Answer: fruits, vegetables, and seeds.) What are some of your favorite fruits, vegetables, and seeds? (Answers will vary.)

2. Does this mean we can't eat anything else? (Answer: No. God has allowed us to eat meat since the flood of Noah.)

3. Meat is an allowance, just as cake or ice cream might be. What are some food allowances you could not do without? (Answers will vary: Doritos, Swedish Fish, peachie rings, brownies…)

SMOOTHIE AND SALAD RECIPES

CREAMY CUCUMBER AND DILL

My mom used to make a version of this for me when I was a kid, and I could not wait for the next time she made it. It's easy enough for your daughter to make it on her own.

1 cucumber, sliced (with or without skin)
1 tsp. dill
1 cup vanilla yogurt
2 T. honey
1 T. vinegar

Mix the last three ingredients. Pour the creamy mixture over the cucumbers and sprinkle with dill.

CARROT RIBBON SALAD

This one is so fun to make. It's a version of the old carrot and raisin salad, but it turns out so much more fun with the carrot ribbons. At some times of the year, you can even get carrots in purple, yellow, and red, not just orange. That makes a really fun salad.

⅔ cup raisins
3–4 carrots
1 cup crushed pineapple, drained
⅓ cup mayonnaise
1 T. lemon juice
½ tsp. salt
1 T. sugar—or make it healthy using a
few dashes of agave

Peel the carrots and then use the peeler to create ribbons. Stir the carrot ribbons, pineapple, and raisins in a bowl. Mix the last four ingredients thoroughly and drizzle over the top. Yum!

TACO SALAD

Ease into healthy eating by having a simple taco salad night. You both get to compile your own salad, but encourage her to try some of the extra-healthy stuff. I usually avoid iceberg lettuce even though it's so yummy—the darker greens are much healthier. But sometimes for taco salad I cave and buy the iceberg.

1 package prewashed salad greens
1 lb. cooked ground beef or ground turkey
with taco seasoning
1 tomato, diced
1 avocado, sliced
1 opened can of black beans, unheated
1 8-oz. package of shredded cheddar cheese
salsa
sour cream or ranch dressing

Set out the ingredients and have fun building your own taco salad.

BLUEBERRY BRANIAC

This is a serious smoothie! It includes ingredients known to help with brain function. Your daughter will like it if she loves blueberries and almonds, which are the two strongest flavors.

1 cup frozen blueberries
1 cup juice (apple, pomegranate,
white grape, or grape works best)
1 T. wheat germ
¼ cup almonds
1 avocado, pitted and peeled

Blend in a high-powered blender. Makes two small smoothies. Bottoms up!

QUICK-AND-EASY
STRAWBERRY BANANA SMOOTHIE

1½ cups orange juice
1 ripe medium banana, peeled and sliced
1 cup frozen strawberries or raspberries
½ cup milk or Silk
2 ice cubes, crushed
1 T. sugar or a dash of agave

Blend and serve. Super easy and fast version of a kid-proven favorite. This smoothie is dairy free if you use Silk.

EXERCISE, YOUR STRENGTH

My sweet Autumn came to us when she was thirteen. But she looked more like she was nine.

Her little body was rail thin, her face was splotchy, and she had a spinal column that looked as if it wanted to give out. She walked and sat in a constant state of slumped dejection. It seemed to me she was struggling with more than just life's hardship. Her little body wasn't strong enough to hold her bowling ball of a head up.

I was right. A visit to the doctor told us she was in the bottom 3 percent of weight for her height and age. That head was one heavy skull for the tiny body sitting under it. We needed to beef up our little China doll. And fast. She was bordering on malnutrition.

My plan would have been to sit her in a room and feed her until she couldn't eat any more, but the doctor explained she needed muscles, not just body fat. He prescribed a good, healthy exercise program to go along with vitamins and a nutrition plan.

Running? She said no.

Walking the dog? She did it unhappily.

Joining me for a workout? No appeal.

Soccer? She loved it!

After just one season of playing middle school soccer and eating nutritious meals, Autumn Gresh had healthy skin, her weight was where it should be, she was carrying her head higher, and she had some great memories to carry too.

It just took us a while to figure out what kind of exercise she would like.

How's your body feeling today? Stretched and toned and strong? Or aching with pain and stress and tension?

Somewhere in my kids' late elementary school years, I realized that my body hurt. Not that good hurt you get from a great workout, but the kind you get from sitting too much. Indulge me an explanation so I can maintain a twinge of my dignity.

In college, I was faithful to work out about five times a week. (Never mind that I stopped by Mom & Pop's Dairy Shop for a milkshake on the way back to my dorm! Hey, it's an "allowance." See conversation five.) When baby number one was born, I tried to work out, but it was only once or twice a week. Then came baby number two. Exercise? Who needs it when you have a toddler and a crawling baby to run after. They *are* an exercise routine.

Gradually, as the kids grew older, I just became less active.

Our girls can fall into the same slump. Until your daughter's tween years, she is most likely naturally active, and it's been all you could do to keep up with her and any siblings she may have. But as our children gradually embrace a more mature, sedentary lifestyle, it's easy to fall into the same pit. And a pit it is. If you don't take care of your body, you won't be strong enough to do all God has for you to do.

And the same is true for her.

Beginning now, I could write a journal article on the benefits of exercise. I could throw mantras at you: "I'm one workout away from feeling great." (That one got me out of bed at six thirty earlier this week to go hit the gym with a small group from my church!) However, I don't really want you to exercise because you're going to look better or feel more positive. Something much more important is at stake. Exercise is a spiritual discipline.

The apostle Paul wrote this about discipline: "The desires of the flesh are against the Spirit, and the desires of the Spirit are against the flesh, for these are opposed to each other, to keep you from doing the things you want to do" (Galatians 5:17).

A battle is raging between your flesh and the Spirit of the living God. Two teachers I have enjoyed, Jenny and Taylor Gallman, once put it this way: Your flesh and your spirit (which houses God's Spirit) are like two sumo wrestlers. The one you feed the most will always be stronger and will always win. Feeding your spirit and calling your flesh into servitude and submission in little things assure you that you'll win in the big things. And the stakes are high.

Paul continues,

> But if you are led by the Spirit, you are not under the law. Now the works of the flesh are evident: sexual immorality, impurity, sensuality, idolatry, sorcery, enmity, strife, jealousy, fits of anger, rivalries, dissensions, divisions, envy, drunkenness, orgies, and things like these. I warn you, as I warned you before, that those who do such things will not inherit the kingdom of God (Galatians 5:18-22).

Our flesh does not naturally desire to do things that glorify God but will easily work to dishonor him. Left to our own devices, we sleep in instead of getting up to read the Word. We watch Netflix programming that trains our mind to laugh at sexual humor rather than to honor the marriage bed. We indulge in too much alcohol rather than having the conviction of self-control...and the list goes on and on. Instead of glorifying God with our bodies, we do a great deal to deny him. What I want you and your daughter to realize during this conversation is this:

> Your spirit has a job to do—to glorify God—so your body better get its attitude straight!

During the seasons when I'm beating my body into submission—getting up to read the Word, saying no to the donuts (or at least to the second one), and exercising regularly—my spirit is in control and able to use my body to glorify God. When my spirit is practicing self-control and overriding my body in these little things, I seem able to win the big battles of temptation much more easily. When I let my flesh have control—and I do sometimes—my ability to glorify God is at risk.

Your daughter is about to enter some of the riskiest years of her life. The list from Galatians includes things that many teenagers fall for—drunkenness, jealousy, fits of anger, envy, rivalries…why, this passage could be the opening credits for a new mean-girls movie!

Help her to win the battles ahead by teaching her that her spirit is in control of her body and not the other way around. (If you need a refresher course, enjoy it, my friend. I'm enjoying one myself as I write this!)

Here's a sample conversation you could use as you discuss this topic with your daughter. Have this conversation while you are hiking or after you exercise if your workout is not conducive to conversation.

Mom: Do you like exercise?

Daughter: (Answers will vary.)

Mom: (Tell your daughter how you feel about exercise and what practical needs you may have for it—weight management, stress management, socialization, and so on.) But the most important reason to exercise has to do with being self-controlled so I can obey God and glorify him with my life. Otherwise, my body just likes to be in charge. I want to sleep in when I need to get up early or eat a lot of pizza at bedtime just because I'm bored. Do you ever feel like that?

Daughter: (Answers will vary.)

Mom: First Corinthians 9:27 says, "I discipline my body and keep it under control." Exercising helps me to discipline my body. You see, if my body is the temple of God (remember when we talked about that?), then I need to make sure it's not in charge, but that God's Spirit is! That means my spirit has to be in charge of my body and not the other way around.

This can be hard to understand, but I learned something recently that gave me a good word picture. Your body and your spirit (which houses God's Spirit) are like two sumo wrestlers. The one you feed the most will always be stronger and will always win. When your body wants to sleep in late but your spirit knows you have to get up to take care of yourself before school, your flesh and your spirit will fight each other. If you let your spirit win, it's like you just fed it! But staying in bed feeds your body. You have to discipline your body to keep it under control. Can you think of a time when you didn't feel like doing something but you knew you needed to do it and you were faithful to override your body's desire to blow it off?

Daughter: (Answers will vary. Help her to remember a time if she needs help, but be careful to lead her to it so it's her own discovery.)

Mom: I would really like to help my spirit practice being in charge of my body. What do you say we enter into a one-week agreement? We could discipline our bodies together through exercise and getting up a little earlier to read our Bibles together and have devotions.

This conversation will begin to establish the foundation for helping your daughter build healthy exercise habits so her spirit and not her body is in control. I encourage you and your daughter to enter into a one-week exercise and devotional challenge. Check out the Spirit Versus Body Challenge beginning on page 115. All the devotions come with a daily exercise idea that you and your daughter can do together.

PLANNING CONVERSATION SIX

AN EXERCISE CHALLENGE

Subject: exercise as strength

Setting options: a mountain hike, a beach walk followed by a swim, snowshoeing

Materials you'll need:

- any materials you might need for the specific setting you have chosen (see the shaded box on the next page for ideas)

- this book

Your main goal in this challenge is to experience the thrills of a good sweat and a quickened heart rate while you talk about why they are important. Select something that will ease your daughter into exercise and will be fun for her. To get you started, I've provided a sidebar of seasonal ideas that involve walking. Select the option that is best for you or select another cardio activity that you can enjoy together. Collect your materials and set out for some fun.

For the best results in this conversation, use *It's Great to Be a Girl*. Do meditation 6 together. If you don't have that book, you can discuss these things.

1. Read 1 Corinthians 9:27. What did the apostle Paul say he did to his body in this verse? And what does that mean? (Answer: Discipline. It means to teach control.)

2. What are some things you can do to train your body to be obedient to God? (Answers will vary. May include getting out of bed on time, exercising, eating right, choosing to obey God when I don't feel like it, and so on.)

3. What are some things you'd like accountability with because you struggle with your body being in control? Anything with food or maybe your schedule? (Answers will vary. Be careful not to lead her. Let her spirit do that work—and the Spirit!)

HIKING CHALLENGE IDEAS

MOUNTAIN HIKE

Hiking is a tremendous aerobic activity that gets your heart pumping and strengthens your muscles. It burns calories and can help with weight loss. The cocktail of chemicals that wash over your brain includes adrenaline and endorphins that might cause you to actually feel more energetic after the walk.

You'll feel it in your calf muscles, glutes, hamstrings, and quads the next day, so match your pace to you and your daughter's current level of physical activity.

- Not very active: Select a slow incline and schedule a short walk.

- Very active: Take on something more challenging and give yourself a little more time. Be sure to take and drink lots of water, especially if you're in higher altitudes.

Materials you need include...

- hiking boots or good-quality sneakers
- water bottles
- an energy snack, such as granola or protein bars

BEACH WALK WITH A SWIM

Walking in the sand burns more calories than walking on the street. Your feet sink into the sand, requiring your muscles to do more work. And the view is extra-beautiful!

You'll need to take a few other precautions in addition to remembering the sunscreen. The sand can create boils on your feet if you walk long distances, so be sure to use good footwear. And because the beach slopes in one direction, the workout on your body can be lop-sided unless you walk halfway in one direction and then turn around and walk the other way. Be sure to stretch because of the extra strain the sand will put on your leg, foot, and glute muscles.

Bonus: Cool off in the water with a quick swim after your walk.

Materials you need include...

- walking shoes or strapped-on walking sandals
- swimwear
- water bottles
- sunscreen

SNOWSHOEING FOR BEGINNERS

Once a survival skill, snowshoeing is now considered a great winter sport. In fact, it's the fastest-growing winter sport and is suitable for all levels of fitness. Just rent or buy a pair of paddle-shaped shoes, strap them on, and enjoy. The benefits of the sport are that it's easy, it poses little risk of injury, and it's a great way to fire up the heart rate during cold winter months. Almost 10 percent of snowshoers are children aged seven to eleven. Don't think that just because it's easy you won't feel the benefits. The sport can burn up to 600 calories an hour. That's 45 percent more than walking or running at the same speed.

By the way, don't be fooled into thinking you can't get sunburned in cold weather. That sun is still strong, and it reflects off the snow!

Materials you need include...

- rented or borrowed snowshoes
- layers of clothing so you can peel some off as your body heats up
- water bottles
- sunscreen

THE SPIRIT VERSUS BODY CHALLENGE

C hallenge yourself each day to enjoy a short devotional together and to exercise. Devotions and exercise ideas for the five-day challenge begin on page 115.

Sign this Spirit Versus Body Challenge. Post it on your fridge or the bathroom mirror so you can both see it every day when you are getting ready for the day.

I discipline my body and keep it under control
(1 Corinthians 9:27).

We, _____ and _____, will attempt to spend _____ minutes a day exercising and will do some quiet prayer and Bible reading before we do it for the next five days. If one of us misses a day, that person will _____ for the other.

Here are some things you can do for each other if you miss more than two days:

- clean the other person's closet
- give her a foot rub and pedicure
- walk the dog when it's her turn
- do the dishes while she relaxes

Signed: _____ Date: _____

Signed: _____ Date: _____

YOUR BODY, A SOURCE OF LIFE

This is the big one, Mom! The conversation everyone wants a book to help with. (But really, none of us really needs an instruction manual. We all know the stork doesn't bring babies!) We'll cover the basic explanation of periods and the necessary ingredient that must accompany their arrival—chocolate, of course. But I'll also give you the prompts to begin a conversation about sexual intercourse in the event that your daughter is ten or older, in which case it is certainly time. You may even find that a younger girl is ready for this part of the conversation.

God created the female body with
the beautiful ability to create life.

I've read material from just about every Christian psychologist or family expert out there, and they all agree that the big sex talk needs to take place much earlier than we parents are generally comfortable having it. Most state that an on-going conversation needs to commence between a child's sixth and tenth year of life.

What happens if you wait? Jimmy Hester, editor of the biblically based *Christian Sex Education*, writes, "By ten or eleven years, many children who have not received adequate instructions about the facts of sexuality become disturbed and worry about what is real. They usually have heard bits and pieces of facts from peers."[15] If they are gaining the first few tidbits of knowledge from peers and other sources, the chances are they are also getting filled with value-laden thoughts about sex, but not the ones you'd like them to have.

Take a deep breath. Don't be surprised if you see words like "vagina," "penis," and "intercourse" straight ahead. You know how it works anyway. I'm just here to offer a little moral support and perhaps to push you off the edge of the conversational cliff in the event you get a case of the nerves. I'm fairly certain you could get through this conversation without my help. After all, you are a mother. You didn't get that way by looking at a man.

Here are a few tips before we begin. I'm introducing you to the way I shared the idea of a period with my girls, and I've really loved the results. They were unafraid, confident, and even able to celebrate the arrival of "*menarche*"—the appropriate name for the first time it happens.

Start with a conversation about the beauty of her body's ability to create life. Back away from the pads and tampons. Let's start in a less obvious place. Why not give it a look right now? Grab your phone and google "photos of babies in utero." Prepare to marvel!

Many moms talk about the basic function of periods but fail to talk about *why* we have them. Your daughter's first period is a sign that God is preparing her to be a mom one day, and it also gives you a wonderful opportunity. You can use your daughter's entrance into womanhood as a value-formation tool concerning the wonder of being a mother.

Next, show her the pictures you found of babies in utero, and accompany them with any of your specific thoughts about carrying her in your womb if you had that honor. I personally had to learn that it's easier than imagined for an adoptive mom to transition to the beauty of the choice her daughter's birth mom made. God will guide you as you gather your thoughts about motherhood.

After you look at these wonderful images, present her with a gift basket or gift bag full of things she'll need for her first period. You can make this to include anything that's important for you and within your value system concerning personal care. Make sure you take time to explain each item and why you included it.

This may be as far as you go during your conversation for now, and that's okay. But don't chicken out if she is ready for more. If she's aged 10 to 12, I can promise you she is.

GIRL THINGZ BASKET IDEAS

mini-pads

regular pads

teen formula pain pills

body spray

chocolate

Thermacare Menstrual Heat Wraps

a note welcoming her to womanhood

Be prepared to answer questions about how that baby gets in there. The good news is that most times, your kids will ask when they are ready to hear the basic mechanics of sexuality. If they are under the age of six, proceed carefully but truthfully. At this age, they are generally not developmentally ready for a brief lesson in conception, but you can answer them by explaining, "A husband and wife often want to show each other how very much they love each other. When they do this, they hold each other in a special way, and I'd like to tell you about that when you're a little older." From there, the conversation should flow into things they are ready for, such as where the baby grows. For example, "After they hold each other in this very special way, a baby often begins to grow inside of the momma! It's a very exciting time for a family."

If your child is over the age of six and especially if she is over the age of nine, it may be time to dig in with the big-picture story.

Be accurate and explicit. Of course, you don't want to be indiscreet or crude. But it's important that you explain the simple facts using real words. You might say something like this.

> When a husband and wife want to show each other how very much they love each other, they use a gift God gave them called sex. They are all alone, and they are naked. God tells us that there is no need to cover their bodies when they are married and that they can enjoy hugging and touching each other. During this time, they hold each other very closely, and the husband can fit his penis into the wife's vagina. This act is God's special way to get the sperm from the man into the woman so that the eggs in her body can be fertilized. This is called intercourse. That's how babies are made.

Be positive if you want to be the continuing expert on sex for your daughter in the years to come. Sex is a great gift from God, and when it is not misused, it is not only pleasurable but also holy! Filling our kids with a negative "don't have sex" message isn't helpful. When they are puzzled by desires as teens or new questions come up, they won't come to you to ask for the answers. They'll turn to sources who have not treated sex as taboo.

How can you be positive now? By communicating the truth that sex is a great gift for a husband and wife—even if your heart has been crushed by sexual sin. God's Word, not our experience, is the standard of truth. And he says that sex is good. Adam and Eve were naked and not ashamed!

While you are enjoying chocolate, have a conversation with your daughter about the beautiful gift God has given women to create life. I won't write this conversation out for you. You will need to develop it based on your daughter's age and readiness. You can use some of the content in the earlier part of this chapter to form your own conversation.

Instead of a script, here are some resources I recommend if you'd like the extra support.

Curriculum

Launch into the Teen Years Kit
by Focus on the Family

Though not entirely about sex, this dynamic video-based series sets you up for six meaningful conversations and experiences with your children including one entitled The Big Talk.

Books

God's Design for Sex series
by Stan and Brenna Jones

Straight Talk with Your Kids About Sex
by Josh and Dottie McDowell

These books will be great tools that make the conversation thorough and easy. Stan and Brenna Jones's books include cartoon graphics of body parts and babies.

PLANNING CONVERSATION SEVEN

DEATH BY CHOCOLATE

Subject: periods and (possibly) sex

Setting options: a chocolate factory, a fondue restaurant, or a chocolate fountain at home

Materials you'll need:

- Ingredients for your own chocolate night at home, if you choose that option. (See the shaded box on the next page for chocolate recipe ideas.)

- a gift basket or bag filled with tampons, pads, pain relievers, body patches, and chocolate

- photos of baby in utero (can be found online)

- this book

For the best results, use *It's Great to Be a Girl.* Do meditation 7 together. If you do not have that book, you can discuss these things.

1. Read John 16:21. Does having a baby hurt? (Answer: Yes. It's a lot of work for a body to do.) Does a mother remember the pain? (Answer: No. She forgets it and only remembers the joy. You might explain how this has worked in your own life.)

2. How are you feeling about getting your period in the next few years? (Answers will vary. Help her focus on the positive gift of her cycle.)

3. Do you have any more questions about how your body creates life? (This is important regardless of whether you have

already had the sex talk. It may be the prompt she needs to ask what she's really thinking. If you have had the talk, it may make her feel comfortable asking questions about it. You want to be the authority on all things related to gender and sex, so make sure she knows she can ask anything at any time.)

CHOCOLATE DATE IDEAS AND RECIPES

CHOCOLATE FACTORY

Visit a small chocolate boutique or a large chocolate factory and learn about chocolate. Be sure to enjoy tastetesting. Take a bag home to share with Dad.

CHOCOLATE FONDUE
AT A RESTAURANT

Restaurants like the Melting Pot have killer fondue. Be make sure to make a reservation.

CHOCOLATE CAMPFIRE

If the weather is nice, you could consider lighting a campfire and making s'mores for this date. Here's my tip for the world's best s'more. Find a clean rock and place it near the heat of the fire. Put your graham cracker and chocolate on the rock so the chocolate warms and softens while you are roasting your marshmallow. Be careful it doesn't turn to liquid chocolate. Yum!

BUDGET CRUNCHER

If you want a more affordable option for chocolate night, pick a fun chocolate activity or recipe to do with your daughter. You'll get another night in the kitchen to build up her skills and you'll have lots of privacy for the conversation.

CHOCOLATE MUFFINS

Make this easy recipe and enjoy the muffins while they are warm so the chocolate chips are gooey.

½ cup butter
½ cup superfine sugar
2 eggs
1 cup self-rising flour
2 tsp. cocoa powder
1 tsp. baking soda
6 oz. chocolate chips

Preheat oven to 350°. Grease 6 muffin cups or place 6 muffin papers in a tin. Cream butter and sugar together in a mixing bowl. Mix in eggs. Add flour, cocoa powder, and baking soda and blend. Fold in chocolate chips. Spoon batter into muffin cups. Bake 15–20 minutes or until toothpick inserted into the center comes out clean. Cool before eating. (At least a little bit, anyway.)

NONEDIBLE CHOCOLATE SLIME

Okay, you can't eat this, but you're sure going to want to. It smells great. I found it on funathomewithkids.com. The recipe is similar to one I've used many times for an object lesson in which I make "sticky situations" fun. I think it could be argued that this conversation on baby makin' could get sticky. Why not also have fun?

2 4-oz. containers clear, washable school glue

Sta-Flo brand liquid starch (an equal amount to glue, so fill up the bottles after they are empty)

3 T. unsweetened cocoa powder

⅛ tsp. brown food coloring or liquid water colors

Mix glue, cocoa powder, and brown food coloring or water color. Fill the glue bottles with Sta-Flo brand liquid starch. Slowly add ½ bottle of the liquid starch to your mixture at a time. Stir well between each addition. Once the slime no longer sticks to the sides of the bowl, reach in and start kneading it by hand. If it sticks to your hands, add liquid starch until it is slippery but not sticky. It will become slimy and stretchy and lots of fun to play with. Store in Ziploc bags. It will last for a few weeks.

YOUR BODY, A SACRIFICE

My first baby came with a bonus experience—panic attacks.

The first one caught me off guard.

During a late-night feeding, I realized my life was never going to be the same again. This child was going to control everything, including my sleep. I would never be alone again, or so I thought. Overwhelmed by the responsibility of it all, I burst into tears and woke my husband with no small amount of heaving. A moist mess, I could barely get the words out to explain what was wrong. Frankly, I didn't know.

Fast-forward three and a half years to baby number two.

I saw it coming.

Instead of bursting into tears when the anxiety rose high into my throat, I quietly walked to the bathroom, closed the door, and prayed.

"Lord, I feel overwhelmed by all you're asking of me, but you have entrusted this little baby girl to me. Help me to know the joy of sacrificing myself, my plans, and my time for this assignment. Quiet the enemy's attempts to fuel selfishness through anxiety and fear. In Jesus' name, amen."

I don't remember ever crying when these bouts of stress hit me after my daughter's birth the way they did with my son. I realize some women need more help than God graced me with in my need, but I remember one thing—I was still stressed.

And I remember praying a lot in that bathroom. It's where I began to learn the truth of sacrificing my body.

Let's review a few of our core thoughts as we land on the last one:

- Every human is created in God's image (Genesis 1:26-27).

- Your daughter's primary *purpose* is to glorify God (1 Corinthians 6:20).

- Your daughter's primary *practice*, then, must be to look like him, and we do that best in the context of distinctive maleness or femaleness (Genesis 1:26-27).

- Your daughter's body, therefore, must be a living sacrifice to God (Romans 12:1-2).

In just a few short years (or maybe a few short months), your daughter will be a teenager and will struggle with increasingly difficult lies about her body, gender, and sexuality. I'd like to finish our time together by looking at the hard truth that glorying God requires sacrifice. Let me review what I shared with you in the first chapter of this book—but this time, from your daughter's perspective.

Ultimately, God gets to choose how we live out the practice of glorifying him. This has been a tremendous blessing in my life, but it has not been without sacrifice.

When my children were young, I wasn't a working mom who had clearly defined work hours, but I wasn't a stay-at-home mom without a job either. God had put in my heart a desire to be an author and I was juggling this calling between childcare and housekeeping. The result was that I was a little lonely. I never really fit into one category—working mom or stay-at-home mom. Many of my working friends enjoyed lunch breaks together. Many of my nonworking friends enjoyed play dates and took naps when their kids did. I was writing books while my children played contentedly or napped, often making up for lost time when they were put to bed at night. I sacrificed social time to be obedient to God as both a mother and author.

My friend Holly obeyed the Lord by allowing him to choose the number of children she would have with her husband, who is a pastor. It ended up being eight! I recently asked her when she had time for devotions and prayer so she could remain a strong mentor to the women God entrusted her to disciple in her church. Her answer—midnight and beyond. She told me that after she nursed the youngest baby at midnight and put him or her down to bed, she opened her Bible for some time of refreshing. Holly sacrificed sleep to be both a faithful mother and a pastor's wife.

My friend Laurel, one of our former board members, obeyed the Lord by leaving a very high-paying, high-powered position in the corporate world when God called her to stay home to be a full-time wife and mom. Not all moms are called to this, and not all moms can do it, but Laurel was called, and her husband had a career that enabled her to quit her job. Her sacrifice included putting her career on hold for many years—possibly two decades—to focus on being a faithful mother and to use her skills in volunteer positions, including serving on my board.

Surely, you're thinking of your own struggles and sacrifice right about now. Some faced bravely with much strength and others faced with a tantrum or two. (I'm not immune.)

Being faithful to glorify God in our bodies as women requires sacrifice.

I would like you to infuse this truth into your daughter at a young age. God is the one who gets to decide how we work, live, give, spend, marry, and worship. Not us.

Early in this book, I shared with you some of the research that

Nancy DeMoss Wolgemuth and I uncovered concerning teen girls before writing *Lies Young Women Believe*. One of the most prevalent lies Christian teen women tend to embrace is that "having a career outside the home is more valuable and fulfilling than being a wife and a mom." These two roles have come under increasing attack in our culture. And the church is not helping our daughters embrace the idea of letting God, not the culture, set the course for their lives. In 1987, only 20 percent of Christians felt that women should not emphasize the roles of being wives and moms. By 2007, 47 percent felt that we should not emphasize the roles of marriage and motherhood for our daughters. I find this to be a tragic change. I would gladly give up my career as an author—with the Lord's permission—to be wife to Bob and mother to my three children.

Here's the good news. What your daughter does now will affect her future. So teach her now that sacrifice is critical, and she'll live it out as you and I have learned to do.

Everyone's career requires sacrifice. Perhaps none more than that of a mom! But your daughter sees that every day, so let's get her into the shoes of someone with a different career that would interest her. (I know that sounds contrary to the purpose of this conversation, but stick with me. I'm headed somewhere.) Our goal in this career date challenge will be to help your daughter begin to internalize the truth that her body is a living sacrifice for God. He gets to call the shots.

You have two goals during this challenge. The first is to introduce your daughter to an exciting career that may interest her in the future. The second (and more important) purpose is to introduce her to the act of sacrificing her body in obedience to God's calling on her life.

PLANNING CONVERSATION EIGHT

A CAREER DATE CHALLENGE

Subject: Your body should be a living sacrifice.

Setting options: the workplace of someone whose career interests your daughter (a veterinarian's office, a horse barn, a church children's department, a fire station, a gym...)

Materials you'll need:

- an appointment with a person whose career would be of interest to your daughter
- a notepad with questions written in it (see below)
- this book

Schedule an appointment for her to shadow someone whose career would be of interest to her. After she's had a nice tour of the work area and helped to sell a car, saddle a horse, paint a wall, or whatever, let her sit down to interview the person she's shadowing. You will have already written these questions into a notebook so she can ask them and take notes.

What is your favorite thing about your career?

What is your least favorite thing about your career?

How do you prepare or care for your body for this field of work?

What sacrifices have you made in the past for this career?

What sacrifices do you continue to make for this career?

For the best results, use *It's Great to Be a Girl*. Do meditation 8 together. If you do not have that book, you can discuss these things.

1. Discuss the interview, focusing on the sacrifices the person has made and will continue to make. (Answers will vary, but in my own career-ministry calling, sacrifices include working on weekends or holidays to meet deadlines, getting up as early as 3:00 a.m. to catch flights to speak somewhere, and being away from home for long periods of time. I have to take care of my body by exercising—otherwise, using a computer strains my neck. I also have to eat right, or I don't have the energy I need to get up early and travel. Taking care of my body is part of the sacrifice because I don't like to exercise and control my eating, but I know that I must to be healthy.)

2. Read Romans 12:1-2. What does it mean to be a "living sacrifice"? (Answer: It means to give things up like sleep, free time, or hobbies so you can be disciplined and obedient.)

3. How can you—as a tween girl—practice being a living sacrifice today so that you can be obedient to God in the career he will call you to someday? (Answers will vary but may include helping you wash the dishes when you ask me, keeping my room clean so I can find things, finishing my homework before I watch television, and getting up early enough to take care of my body before school—brushing my teeth, brushing my hair, taking a bath if I need it, and so on.)

4. *Most important question*: Do you know what my career is? (Answer may be "mom," or she may mention a career you have outside the home. Either way, take this time to tell her that your career as a wife and mom is the most important thing you do. That you love it more than any other career you've ever had and you'd happily be wife and mom at the expense of all the other careers in the world. Explain to her the sacrifices you have made for this. Infuse her with passion for the greatest career in the world—mom.)

SPIRIT VERSUS BODY CHALLENGE

Use this five-day challenge in conjunction with
chapter 9, conversation 6—"Exercise, Your Strength."

SPIRIT

Walking with God

Bible blast—read Galatians 5:16-25

If we live by the Spirit, let us also walk by the Spirit.

GALATIANS 5:25

Trigg is the world's sweetest horse and my lifelong dream come true. Since I was a girl, I wanted a horse and dreamed he might be a palomino, and he is one of the most beautiful of palominos. He has a deep-copper-colored body, which contrasts against his light blond mane. I once wrote that his eyes are warm and inviting with ink-black skin around them that is soft like velvet. He's a Tennessee walker, so he has a smooth and steady gait and is really fun to ride.

My boy is happy to take me out on trail rides, where we see wild turkey take to flight, deer bouncing through the cornfields, and the occasional sly fox. Nothing disturbs his confident and strong stride. He was made for the trail. These rides are so very peaceful...well, on the way out at least.

But on the way home, *he* likes to be in charge of everything. Which way we come home and how fast. When we stop for a nibble of wheat and when we trot or canter...or gallop. His once-gentle temperament goes 100 percent stubborn on me, and he pulls at the bit no matter how much it hurts him. For three years I've been teaching him to let me control *all* of our trail rides. He doesn't like it.

But I love him still.

When you go on a walk with someone, you have to make a lot of decisions. First, you decide where you will go. Second, you decide which way to go because there may be more than one way to get there.

Then as you begin walking, you decide how fast or slow you will walk. You even decide when to turn around if you are returning the same way. Someone has to be in charge.

Today's key Bible verse invites us to walk with God's Spirit.

If you are walking with God's Spirit, who do you think gets to be in charge?

Yep, he gets to decide where we go, how we get there, and how fast.

Trigg reminds me of myself. When God invites me on an adventure, I'm obedient—in the beginning. I pray a lot and let him be in charge. But soon I find myself acting like Trigg and pulling at the reins. Or I'm happy to let God decide where the next adventure might take me as long as I get to be in charge of all the details. I'm not good at letting God lead in the details of our walk.

Recently, he's been teaching me to listen to him for *all* the directions. Even the littlest of things. I'm not always as obedient and agreeable as I want to be, but I'm confident of this—even when I act like Trigg on the way home and pull at the bit, God still loves me.

His love calls me to be a better walker.

GIRL GAB

Mom, share about how hard it sometimes is to let God be in control of your daily walk. Be specific.

Daughter, talk to your mom about learning to walk with God's Spirit. What does that mean for you this week, and how will you do it?

BODY

Walk and Talk

Grab your mom for a good ol' walk and talk. Walking is a great cardio activity. (That means your heart gets a workout, not just your legs!) And talking increases the work that your lungs and heart do. You intensify the benefits of the walk if you're talking while you do it.

Time Goal

Try to walk for 20 minutes.

SPIRIT

Running with Endurance

Bible blast—read Hebrews 12:1-2

Let us run with endurance the race that is set before us.

HEBREWS 12:1

In all the animal kingdom, basilisks may have the most amazing running ability of all. They literally run for their lives!

Living in Mexico and Central and South America, these lizards gravitate to water—and with good reason. When threatened by predators, they jump into protective mode and race across the water at the speed of five feet per second. They aren't very big, so those little feet of theirs are surely moving faster than ours can. In fact, they're so fast that they walk on water for about 15 feet, giving them a unique nickname. Since Jesus is the only person who has walked on water, the locals call these little guys "Jesus Christ" lizards.

What happens after they reach fifteen feet? Gravity takes over, and they begin to sink. But they do not give in. They keep going! The 15 feet of running gives them a head start, and they start swimming with all their might. These scaly guys are not quitters. They endure.

The word "endure" can mean two things. First, it can mean to remain in existence or to last (which is what the lizards do). Second, it can mean to suffer. Either way, you're looking at some serious commitment.

When it comes to running, I am kind of like the basilisk. I run only when something wants to eat me!

But my coauthor and former True Girl lead teacher Suzy Weibel loves running. Well, she didn't always. She started running because she

121

saw people around her getting so fit and healthy by doing it. It made her want to endure—to last and to suffer—until she was also fit and healthy. Now she says that the way she feels after a run is worth the endurance. I may never know, but it inspires me to endure in the workouts I enjoy a lot. (More on that in a future devotion.)

When God writes about running with endurance in the book of Hebrews, he is talking about our faith, not our feet. He is telling us that you have to make a choice in order to be a faith-runner and that it will require you to have lasting power. You may get weary at times, but don't give up. Don't quit.

As I run to stay fit in the faith, sometimes I don't feel like getting up early to have devotions. Or sometimes I feel like it will be too much work to share my faith with someone. There are even times when I doubt God. (Thankfully, some of the most faithful characters in the Bible struggled with that too, so I'm not alone.) When the times of weariness and doubt come, I remember this verse, strap on a little extra dose of endurance, and run on.

How about you? What will you decide?

GIRL GAB

Talk about what it means to be a faith runner. What does God require of you that might mean lasting long or even suffering? Pray for each other that you'll be faithful to endure!

BODY

One Mile Run–Walk

Running isn't easy if you're just starting, but I've learned that even I am able to enjoy a good run–walk. I set my goal of how long or how far I want to run, and then I run as long as I can. When I grow too tired, I don't quit. Instead, I walk until I feel my stamina return. In this way, I endure. Set a goal to run one mile today. Walk some of it if you need to, but endure until the end.

Time Goal

The fastest people in the world finish a mile in about four minutes. Average, seasoned runners usually take seven to ten minutes. If it's your first time, allow 10 to 15 minutes.

SPIRIT

Don't Keep Score

Bible blast—read 1 Corinthians 13

*[Love] does not dishonor others, it is not self-seeking,
it is not easily angered, it keeps no record of wrongs.*

1 CORINTHIANS 13:5 NIV

The highest soccer game score in all of history was 149–0. In a game where a score of 20–0 is considered an unbelievable blowout, this seems an impossible score.

And so it was.

Apparently, a referee had upset the coach and players of the *Stade Olympique de l'Emyrne* team during a championship match in Madagascar. The coach staged a most unusual protest. The team got control of the ball and starting scoring *for the other team*! One after another, they put the goal in their own net. The opposing team didn't even know what to do. With both teams working to get the goal into one net, it was no contest.

The thing is, it was a rebellion against the authorities. And those authorities didn't like it one bit. The end result was that the coach was not allowed to coach for three years, and two key players were suspended for a year. The rest of the team members got fines and warnings. If they'd known what the cost would be, they might not have run up the score the way they did.

Keeping score in sports is a fun and fair way to play a game, but anger and resentment in the players' hearts take away the contest. And the fun.

God instructs you and me not to keep score in real-life relationships. First Corinthians 13:5 says that if we really love someone, we will not keep any record of wrongs.

Corrie ten Boom gave us a great example of this kind of love. Corrie was imprisoned in a concentration camp during World War II simply because her family assisted Jews. She watched Nazi soldiers treat people she loved badly, she lived in a bunkhouse infested with fleas, and she practically starved to death. Her sister died in that camp, and her father died in a similar one. When the war was over, Corrie traveled around the world, encouraging people who'd survived the war to love others in a way that "keeps no record of wrongs."

Her message was put to the test one night when one of the soldiers who'd mistreated her showed up at one of her church services. After she spoke, he approached her and thanked her, explaining that it felt so good to be forgiven for the awful things he'd done to people. Corrie realized that he did not recognize her because she was clean and well-fed. God was asking her to practice what she preached. This act of forgiveness was one of the most difficult things she ever did, and for a moment she did not know if she could do it. But then she reached out her hand and shook his as an act of love. By God's strength she did it. She kept no record of this man's wrongs.

If Corrie could forgive a man who helped orchestrate her suffering and the death of her sister and father, you and I can forgive those who have wronged us.

Let's stop keeping score.

Unless it's a *fair* game of soccer!

GIRL GAB

Mom, share with your daughter a time when it was very difficult to forgive a friend in middle school or high school.

Daughter, talk to your mom about someone you're having trouble forgiving right now.

Pray that God would help you both to keep no record of wrongs.

BODY

One-on-One Soccer

Grab a soccer or kick ball and set up two goals. Have an aggressive game of one-on-one soccer. Keep score but play fair! If your family is around, you might make this a family match!

Time Goal

Play for about 20 minutes if you are playing one-on-one.
If you play with a larger team, stretch that out to
40 minutes because you'll have more resting time.

SPIRIT

Firmly Planted Feet

Bible blast—read Ephesians 6:10-20

Put on the whole armor of God, that you may be able to stand against the schemes of the devil.

EPHESIANS 6:11

The only competitive sport I truly enjoy playing is tennis. (And interestingly, it's kind of a cooperation as much as competition. As two players work together to keep the ball in play, they are also trying to make it difficult for the other person to do so. In some crazy way, it takes teamwork to be competitive.) I just love the sound of that ball bouncing on the court, and there's nothing like the smell of a new can of neon-yellow Wilsons!

One thing I learned in my tennis class is that you will never win the game if you don't learn to stand with your feet firmly planted on the court when you hit the ball. Many players spend all their time developing their stroke or focusing on their equipment (shoes, racket, headband, wrist bands…), but the big winners are the ones who focus on their stance. When you see a good game on television, you might never guess that they aren't moving all the time. But the truth is that unless you learn the "ready stance" and practice planting your feet when you hit the ball, you'll never get any power behind your stroke. And, oh, the pop of that ball when you have power in the swing!

God wants us to have our feet firmly planted in our spiritual battles too.

Ephesians 6 describes the spiritual armor of God, which we are supposed to wear to protect ourselves from the devil and his bad plans for us. As in tennis, you need not only to put on the right equipment (belt of truth, breastplate of righteousness, sword of truth, and so on) but also to stand with your feet firmly planted. In fact, the passage uses the word "stand" three times just to make sure we really understand that no matter how afraid we may be of something, God calls us to stand our ground.

When I first started speaking in front of tween and teen girls, I was terrified. I knew God had called me into the battle of protecting your heart and mind, but I didn't like speaking out loud. I'm rather shy. But God called me to stand firm. To be brave and to trust him to take care of the details. I'm still a little shy and sometimes afraid to speak in public, but not like I used to be. In standing my ground, I gained courage.

Is there anything you are afraid of doing that you feel God is asking you to do?

Stand strong!

GIRL GAB

Mom, share a story of a time when you had to stand your ground even though you felt afraid. How did you feel after you did it?

Daughter, tell your mom what makes you fearful. Is it speaking in front of people, introducing yourself to new friends, or going to a youth group for the first time?

Pray together that you would both learn to plant your feet and stand!

BODY

Tennis

Borrow some rackets if you must, but hit the tennis courts today. Remember to plant your feet firmly while you are waiting for the other person to hit the ball (this is called a ready stance) and when you hit the ball. For more specific instructions on this, you can google "how to play tennis." Enjoy!

Time Goal

Play for about 30 minutes.

SPIRIT

Self-Control

Bible blast—read 1 Corinthians 9:24-27

I discipline my body and keep it under control, lest after preaching to others I myself should be disqualified.

1 CORINTHIANS 9:27

n the year 2013, the World's Strongest Man competition was held in China. The media staged a fun activity with the competitors. It was watermelon harvest season, so they took the men out to haul baskets of several watermelons—one in each hand—weighing up to 110 pounds each. Picture this—a huge basket on each side of a guy with up to eight watermelons per basket! A huge crowd gathered to watch and marvel at these strong men.

Suddenly, out of the group came a small, middle-aged Asian woman. Compared to these huge body builders, she looked like a child. She simply picked up two baskets and started walking. As she did she said, "This is nothing. We do this all the time." Carrying the baskets was easy for her because she worked like that every day. You can see a picture of her by googling "World's strongest men stunned by female farmer in China."

Strength training is a big deal in the athletic world. It includes any exercise that focuses on muscle resistance to build control and strength. Examples include weight lifting, Pilates, or short calisthenics (such as pull-ups and sit-ups). Some people think it's not as fun because it's not active or competitive, but I really enjoy the quiet focus that a Pilates workout offers. You might too. But the real reason most people do it is that it builds strong muscles and protects you from injury when you do other kinds of exercise. It enables you to compete more successfully in ball games or speed-based races, such as biking or running.

God's Word instructs us to be like athletes who practice self-control and discipline. The apostle Paul wrote, "I discipline my body and keep it under control, lest after preaching to others I myself should be disqualified." Discipline requires doing things we don't like or prefer. But in doing those things, we develop the freedom to run the race of our faith more effectively. What are some examples of this?

Well, I don't really like memorizing Bible verses, for example. But doing this is kind of like strength training. I'm developing something I'll need and use in the real game of the faith. So I memorize Bible verses. Recently, I've been asking God to make me more faithful and effective with this—it's really difficult work for my brain.

What's hard for you to do?

Do it to be a disciplined follower of Christ.

GIRL GAB

Mom, tell your daughter what's difficult for you to do in terms of training yourself to be spiritually strong.

Daughter, tell your mom the same thing.

Commit to encourage each other in those things. And pray to ask God for his encouragement too.

BODY

Strength Training

Today, I'd like you to try some strength training. You can google "online Pilates workout" for some videos that guide you through a Pilates workout, head to the gym with Mom for some weight lifting (make sure you have help to do it safely and correctly), or just get in the backyard and do several sets of push-ups, sit-ups, and pull-ups! Discipline your body so it can compete in other games.

Time Goal

Strength train for 10–20 minutes.

NOTES

Chapter 1: Why Your Daughter Needs Body Confidence

1. Deborah Swaney, "Fast Times: When did 7 become the new 16?" *Family Circle*, November 29, 2008, p. 48.

2. Eileen L. Zurbriggen et al., *Report of the APA Task Force on the Sexualization of Girls*, www.apa.org /pi/women/programs/girls/report-full.pdf.

3. Stacy Weiner, "Goodbye to Girlhood," special to *Washington Post*, February 20, 2007, www.one angrygirl.net/goodbyetogirlhood.html.

Chapter 2: Starting with You

4. www.youtube.com/watch?v=Pqknd1ohhT4.

5. Katy Steinmetz, "The Transgender Tipping Point," *Time*, May 29, 2014, time.com/135480 /transgender-tipping-point/.

6. John Piper, "Genitalia Are Not Destiny—but Are They Design?" June 2, 2014, www.desiringgod .org/blog/posts/genitalia-are-not-destiny-but-are-they-design.

Chapter 3: Helping Your Daughter to Be Body Confident

7. Sara A. Divall and Sally Radovick, "Pubertal Development and Menarche," in *The Menstrual Cycle and Adolescent Health*, ed. Catherine M. Gordon et al. (New York: New York Academy of Sciences, 2008), pp. 19-28.

8. James Dobson, *Solid Answers* (Wheaton: Tyndale House, 1997), p. 197.

Chapter 4: Conversation One: Your Body, a Purpose

9. John Piper, *Brothers, We Are Not Professionals* (Nashville: B&H Books, 2013), p. 6.

Chapter 5: Conversation Two: Your Body, Its Practice

10. Lindsay Leigh Bentley, "I Am Ryland—the Story of a Male-Identifying Little Girl Who Didn't Transition," *Lindsay Leigh Bentley* (blog), June 30, 2014, lindsayleighbentley.com/2014 /06/30/i-am-ryland-the-story-of-a-male-identifying-little-girl-who-didnt-transition/.

Chapter 6: Conversation Three: Your Body, God's Temple

11. Cited in "Tween Talk," *Gillette Venus*, www.gillettevenus.com/en-US/venus-beauty/articles /how-to-shave-mom/.

Chapter 8: Conversation Five: Food, Your Fuel

12. Cited in "Childhood Obesity Facts," Centers for Disease Control and Prevention, www.cdc.gov /healthyyouth/obesity/facts.htm.

13. Dannah Gresh, *Six Ways to Keep the "Little" in Your Girl* (Eugene: Harvest House, 2010), pp. 32-33.

14. Statistics cited in "Obesity Prevention Source," Harvard School of Public Health, www.hsph .harvard.edu/obesity-prevention-source/obesity-consequences/health-effects/.

Chapter 10: Conversation Seven: Your Body, a Source of Life

15. Jimmy Hester, ed., *Christian Sex Education* (Nashville: Lifeway, 1995), p. 42

Six Ways to Keep the "Little" in Your Girl

Guiding Your Daughter from Her Tweens to Her Teens

Today's world pressures girls to act older than they are when they're not ready for it. How can you help your tween daughter navigate the stormy waters of boy-craziness, modesty, body image, media, Internet safety, and more?

Dannah Gresh shares six easy ways to help your daughter grow up to be confident, emotionally healthy, and strong in her faith. In a warm and transparent style, Dannah shows you how to…

- help your daughter celebrate her body in a healthy way
- unbrand her when the world tries to buy and sell her
- unplug her from a plugged-in world
- dream with her about her future

Six Ways to Keep the "Good" in Your Boy

Guiding Your Son from His Tweens to His Teens

God created boys to become men who are good—embracing God's call to unselfishly provide and protect. As a mom, you have a unique role in this process.

Dannah Gresh blends thorough analysis of the trends that can impact your son—including porn, aggressive girls, and video games gone overboard—with positive, practical advice you can use effectively to help guide your son toward "good" during the vital ages of 8 to 12. Dannah shows you…

- why a boy needs to play outside
- how reading good books makes him a leader
- what role a mom plays in his entrance into manhood
- tips to keep him unplugged from impurity

*With special insights for dads from Bob Gresh
and for single moms from Angela Thomas*

8 Great Dates for Dads and Daughters

How to Talk About the Differences Between Boys and Girls

Our culture pressures girls to crush on boys way too soon, but a dad's involvement in his daughter's growing interest is her greatest protection.

Bob and Dannah Gresh have created these 8 great dates to help a father and daughter connect on a topic that really matters—and have a terrific time together. (Think: pulling pranks, treasure hunting, and more as you consider God's Word.) You'll tackle big questions from your daughter's point of view…

- What was God thinking when he created girls to like boys?
- Why is everyone boy-crazy? Should I be?
- When can I start to date? (It's not too soon to talk about it!)
- How can I embrace purity?

Here's a simple and complete resource with fresh ways to build your connection with your little girl—and to love and protect her as she grows up.

8 Great Dates for Moms and Daughters

How to Talk About Cool Fashion, True Beauty, and Dignity

Dannah Gresh, founder of True Girl, presents you and your girl with eight unique, interactive mother-daughter dates to deepen your relationship and have meaningful discussions about true beauty, body image, dignity, and more.

The dates are easy to plan, budget-friendly, and fun. You and your girl will enjoy connecting over tea, facials, fashion, and more. These engaging activities also make great group outings, so invite your friends and their daughters to join you and make it a party!

Most important, you'll have valuable opportunities to share biblical truths that affirm your daughter's value in Christ, protect her heart, and help her make sense of her changing body and emotions.

To learn more about Harvest House books and
to read sample chapters, visit our website:

www.harvesthousepublishers.com

HARVEST HOUSE PUBLISHERS
EUGENE, OREGON